AWESOME HOCKEY TRIVIA

GREYSTONE BOOKS
Douglas & McIntyre
Vancouver/Toronto

To hockey trivia fans everywhere. — Don Weekes

Copyright © 1998 by Don Weekes

98 99 00 01 02 5 4 3 2 1

Greystone Books
A division of Douglas & McIntyre
1615 Venables Street
Vancouver, British Columbia   V5L 2H1

Canadian Cataloguing in Publication Data
Weekes, Don.
  Awesome hockey trivia
  ISBN 1-55054-646-5
  1. National Hockey League—Miscellanea. 2. Hockey—Miscellanea. I. Title
GV847.W35 1998   796.962'64   C98-910540-7

Editing by Anne Rose and Kerry Banks
Design by Peter Cocking
Typesetting by Brenda and Neil West, BN Typographics West
Cover photo John Giamundo
Printed and bound in Canada by Best Book Manufacturers
Printed on acid-free paper ∞

The publisher gratefully acknowledges the assistance of the Canada Council for the Arts and of the British Columbia Ministry of Tourism, Small Business and Culture. The publisher also acknowledges the financial support of the Government of Canada through the Book Publishing Industry Development Program for its publishing activities.

Don Weekes *is a television producer and writer with* CFCF *12 in Montreal. This is his eleventh hockey trivia quiz book.*

CONTENTS

PREFACE

Who was the first American-born player to notch three straight 50-goal seasons in the NHL? In more than a century of hockey, only a few Canadians, such as Bobby Hull, Wayne Gretzky and Mike Bossy, have racked up goals so consistently. But, for the first time, Vermonter John LeClair of the Philadelphia Flyers scored his third straight 50th, in 1997-98.

In fact, LeClair and Brett Hull are the only NHLers of the 1990s to record three straight 50-goal years. That fact says as much about the erosion of goal scoring and the improving defensive strategies in play today as it does about the subtle shift away from the once Canadian-dominated scoring race to a truly international free-for-all.

Check out the top-five point earners of 1997-98. All five hailed from different countries, an NHL first. Jaromir Jagr (102 points) from the Czech Republic, led the league, followed by Peter Forsberg (91 points) from Sweden, Pavel Bure (90 points) from Russia, Wayne Gretzky (90 points) from Canada and John LeClair (87 points), an American. Without a doubt, the 1980s and 1990s have proved to be a watershed for American and European players and their hockey systems.

However, those low point totals also reveal how much scoring has declined in the NHL. Aside from the lockout-shortened 1994-95 campaign, you have to turn the clock all the way back to 1969-70 to find a season when only one NHLer compiled 100 points.

In an attempt to rejuvenate scoring and speed up the game, the NHL implemented a crackdown on obstruction fouls in 1997-98 and is considering several other modifications. They include: Not letting the goalie play the puck out of his own crease, eliminating the centre redline, allowing two-line passes, downsizing goalie equipment, enlarging the goalie nets and moving them further from the ends of the boards, and having players serve the full two minutes of minor penalties, regardless of whether the other team scores during its man-power advantage.

Perhaps the best plan, to widen the ice surface to international size to accommodate today's bigger, faster players and open up the game, came too late. The next generation of hockey rinks have already been built at 200 by 85 feet, the same dimensions that old-time teams played on a century ago.

Yet despite its problems, hockey has never been more popular. As long as its essentials—skating, shooting, passing and hard-hitting remain intact, the game should continue to thrive as it evolves into the next century.

In this 11th edition of our ongoing series of hockey trivia books, we test your hockey IQ with the most fascinating stories—everything from famous players to obscure facts.

DON WEEKES
May 1998

Visit my Web site at: **www3.sympatico.ca/don.weekes/**

1

SHOWTIME

Most hockey players are superstitious. Before each game they follow a closely scripted routine for dressing, lacing up and hitting the ice. Sometimes they can get quite inventive in their search for good-luck charms. So when Montreal Canadiens captain Vincent Damphousse glided to centre ice for the ceremonial face-off against the Tampa Bay Lightning in March 1998, he knew exactly what he was about to do. After the puck was dropped by pop music superstar Celine Dion, Damphousse planted a kiss on the lady's cheek. "I wanted some of her talent to rub off on me," Damphousse said. It worked, considering he went on to score a hat trick in the Habs' 8-2 romp over the Lightning.

In this opening face-off on general hockey trivia, may Lady Luck rub a little success into your game plan, too. Remember, it's not just what you know, but how well you pick from the multiple-choice options.

(Answers are on page 6)

1.1 Which NHL city is known as "Hockeytown"?
   A. Toronto
   B. Detroit
   C. New York
   D. Philadelphia

1.2 In what season did Mike Modano record his first 50-goal year?
   A. In 1989-90, his rookie season
   B. In 1990-91, Bob Gainey's first year as coach
   C. In 1993-94, the Stars' first season in Dallas
   D. In 1995-96, Ken Hitchcock's first year as coach

1.3 When Wayne Gretzky scored seven assists on February 15, 1980, he tied an NHL record first set in what decade?
A. The 1940s
B. The 1950s
C. The 1960s
D. The 1970s

1.4 The first player to post a 100-point season was Canadian Phil Esposito. Which country produced the first non-Canadian 100-point player?
A. USA
B. Finland
C. Sweden
D. USSR

1.5 As of 1997-98, who is the highest goal-scoring NHLer not in the Hockey Hall of Fame?
A. Dale Hawerchuk
B. Bryan Trottier
C. Denis Savard
D. Michel Goulet

1.6 Which Pittsburgh Penguin player did Ray Bourque hit in 1997-98, when he received the first game misconduct of his career?
A. Stu Barnes
B. Jaromir Jagr
C. Kevin Hatcher
D. Ron Francis

1.7 During the ensuing Pittsburgh power play, after Ray Bourque received a game misconduct and five-minute penalty for checking from behind (see question above), what scoring milestone was reached by a Penguin player?
A. A rookie goal record
B. A career assist total by a defenseman
C. A career point total by a forward
D. A team goal record

1.8 A select few NHL rookies have scored a point on their first NHL shift. Who did it in the fastest time?
A. Danny Gare of the Buffalo Sabres
B. Mario Lemieux of the Pittsburgh Penguins
C. Bobby Carpenter of the Washington Capitals
D. Wayne Gretzky of the Edmonton Oilers

1.9 Which coach holds the NHL record for most wins in his rookie season behind the bench?
A. Philadelphia's Mike Keenan
B. Boston's Tom Johnson
C. Montreal's Pat Burns
D. Calgary's Doug Risebrough

1.10 Who holds the NHL mark for the most fighting majors in one game?
A. John Ferguson
B. Eddie Shore
C. Dave Schultz
D. Tiger Williams

1.11 Who set a new NHL record by scoring three penalty-shot goals in 1997-98?
A. Vancouver's Pavel Bure
B. Chicago's Tony Amonte
C. Calgary's Theo Fleury
D. St. Louis' Pierre Turgeon

1.12 During the 1980s, Wayne Gretzky won the Hart Trophy as league MVP every year except one. Which season did Gretzky miss, and who spoiled his perfect 10?
A. 1980-81, Marcel Dionne
B. 1984-85, Dale Hawerchuk
C. 1986-87, Ray Bourque
D. 1987-88, Mario Lemieux

1.13 As of 1997-98, who is the only 50-goal scorer traded in midseason to score at least 25 goals for each team during that season?
A. Craig Simpson with Pittsburgh and Edmonton
B. Joe Mullen with St. Louis and Calgary
C. Dave Andreychuk with Buffalo and Toronto
D. Mike Gartner with Minnesota and New York

1.14 As of 1997-98, what is the most number of NHL teams played on by one player?
A. Seven teams
B. Eight teams
C. Nine teams
D. 10 teams

1.15 As of 1997-98, who is the only player in NHL history to record 300 goals and 3,000 penalty minutes?
A. Tiger Williams
B. Dale Hunter
C. Bob Probert
D. Rick Tocchet

1.16 Detroit players gave which fellow Red Wing the nickname "Sam Jones" in 1997?
A. Sergei Fedorov
B. Darren McCarthy
C. Steve Yzerman
D. Nicklas Lidstrom

1.17 Which NHL sniper scored the last regular-season goal of his career on a penalty shot?
A. Mike Bossy
B. Phil Esposito
C. Mario Lemieux
D. Guy Lafleur

1.18 How many seconds into the Avalanche-Red Wings game on
      November 11, 1997, did it take Colorado's Claude Lemieux
      and Detroit's Darren McCarty to start fighting another
      round in their ongoing feud?
      A. Three seconds
      B. 33 seconds
      C. 66 seconds
      D. 99 seconds

1.19 What is the height of the tallest player in North American
      pro hockey?
      A. Six foot six
      B. Six foot eight
      C. Six foot nine
      D. Six foot ten

1.20 In the 1993 NHL draft, Paul Kariya was chosen fourth overall
      (Anaheim), Chris Gratton third (Tampa Bay) and Chris
      Pronger second (Hartford). Who was the first pick, who
      when asked how it felt being chosen said, "Nobody remembers
      who was picked second."?
      A. Roman Hamrlik of the Tampa Bay Lightning
      B. Eric Lindros of the Philadelphia Flyers
      C. Alexandre Daigle of the Ottawa Senators
      D. Ed Jovanovski of the Florida Panthers

1.21 Wayne Gretzky took the fewest games to score 50 goals in a
      season. Which player was the fastest to reach 100 points in a
      season?
      A. Mario Lemieux
      B. Pat LaFontaine
      C. Steve Yzerman
      D. Wayne Gretzky

1.22 Barring a rule change, in which season did the NHL's last
helmetless player score a goal?
A. 1994-95
B. 1995-96
C. 1996-97
D. 1997-98

1.23 How high in altitude is Denver's NcNichols Arena?
A. 2,000 feet above sea level
B. 3,000 feet above sea level
C. 4,000 feet above sea level
D. One mile above sea level

1.24 Who was the first U.S. president to attend an NHL game
while in office?
A. John F. Kennedy
B. Ronald Reagan
C. George Bush
D. Bill Clinton

1.25 Which New York Islander is being checked by Detroit's
Sergei Fedorov in the picture on the front cover of this book?
A. Scott Lachance
B. Zigmund Palffy
C. Robert Reichel
D. Kenny Jonsson

SHOWTIME
Answers

1.1 B. Detroit
If the Red Wings have their way, Detroit won't be called the
"Motor City" or "Motown" much longer. Welcome to "Hockeytown," a five-year marketing campaign launched by the Wings
in 1996 to appeal to "a region full of hockey fans." After the
1996-97 season, Hockeytown had a lot to cheer about, boasting
three champion hockey teams. In addition to the Stanley

Cup-winning Red Wings, the Detroit Vipers won the IHL's Turner Cup; the Plymouth Whalers claimed the OHL junior title. Hockey-crazy Detroit also plays host to numerous college and minor hockey programs.

1.2   C. In 1993-94, the Stars' first season in Dallas
Modano's 30-goal seasons were never good enough for Minnesota fans, who ruthlessly badgered their "pretty boy" for not scoring more or playing a more physical and defensive game. "It was brutal up there," Modano told *The Hockey News*. "The best thing for me was when the team moved [in 1993]." Modano silenced his Minnesota critics in his first Dallas season with 50 goals and 93 points. Under coaches Bob Gainey and later Ken Hitchcock, Modano has developed into a bona fide NHL star.

1.3   A. The 1940s
Although the Great One did it three times during his stellar career, the first and only other seven-assist game in the NHL came courtesy of Billy "The Kid" Taylor. On March 16, 1947, Taylor caught fire, notching seven helpers in Detroit's 10-6 win over Chicago. Thanks to his playmaking skills, Taylor led the league in assists with 46 and finished third in the scoring race. His most-assists-in-a-game record lasted for a remarkable 33 years until equaled by Gretzky. Taylor's other claims to NHL fame are his 1942 Stanley Cup with Toronto and, later, his lifelong suspension from hockey for betting on his own team's games in 1948. (He and Boston linemate Don Gallinger were reinstated in 1970.)

1.4   C. Sweden
Kent Nilsson from Nynasham, Sweden, delivered two 100-point seasons in the WHA before graduating to the NHL, where, unlike most former WHAers, he excelled, scoring 49 goals and 131 points in 1980-81 with the Calgary Flames. Nilsson's historic 100th point, the first by a non-Canadian NHLer, came on February 27, 1981, against Hartford. That season, Nilsson finished third in the scoring race, behind Wayne Gretzky and Marcel

Dionne. Nilsson was the 30th player in league history to score 100 points in a year.

1.5 D. Michel Goulet
In 1997, his first year of eligibility (after the mandatory three-year waiting period), Goulet was not nominated for Hall of Fame status, although he was the highest-scoring NHLer eligible. During his 15-year career with Quebec and Chicago, Goulet scored 548 goals.

1.6 B. Jaromir Jagr
It happened in Bourque's 1,341st regular-season game. The Bruins' defensive stalwart had never been assessed more than 96 penalty minutes in a season and had picked up only two 10-minute misconducts in his illustrious career. But on January 29, 1998, Bourque received a game misconduct—the first ejection of his 19-year career—after hitting Jagr from behind and sending him headfirst into the boards behind the net. Jagr remained on the ice for five minutes but returned in the second period. The Pens beat Boston 4-2.

1.7 C. A career point total by a forward
A little more than a minute into Bourque's checking-from-behind penalty, Stu Barnes connected on a pass from Ron Francis, who earned his 1,400th point. Francis is only the 11th NHLer to reach this milestone.

1.8 C. Bobby Carpenter of the Washington Capitals
The Capitals rookie got his name on an NHL scoresheet in record time, setting up a goal by linemate Ryan Walter against Buffalo netminder Don Edwards, only 12 seconds into his first NHL game, on October 7, 1981.

1.9 B. Boston's Tom Johnson
Coach Tom Johnson was handed the reins of the NHL's best team in his first season; aided by Phil Esposito and Bobby Orr, he won 57 games with the Bruins in 1970-71. Keenan and Burns rank second (each had 53 rookie wins with their respective clubs).

Most Wins by Rookie NHL Coaches*

Coach	Season	Team	GP	W	L	T
Tom Johnson	1970-71	Boston	78	57	14	7
Mike Keenan	1984-85	Philadelphia	80	53	20	7
Pat Burns	1988-89	Montreal	80	53	18	9
Claude Ruel	1968-69	Montreal	76	46	19	11
Toe Blake	1955-56	Montreal	70	45	15	10
Jimmy Skinner	1954-55	Detroit	70	42	17	11
Joe Primeau	1950-51	Toronto	70	41	16	13

Current to 1998

1.10 B. Eddie Shore

In the early days of hockey, players were not limited to the number of fights they could become involved in during a game. That opened the penalty-box door for some rough-and-tumble action. On November 23, 1929, the Bruins' Eddie Shore picked up a record five fighting majors against the Montreal Maroons in a game marred by so much violence that it had to be stopped in the third period in order to scrape blood from the ice. Shore first tangled with the Maroons' George Boucher, then Dave Trottier, Hooley Smith, Red Dutton and finally Babe Siebert. Trottier claimed he was butt-ended by Shore, resulting in a slight lung hemorrhage to the Maroon rookie winger. In the last fracas, Siebert, who suffered a broken toe, bruised rib and black eye thanks to Shore, retaliated by sending Shore to the hospital with a broken nose, a concussion and four missing teeth. Thirteen-year veteran Boucher said it was the roughest game he had ever played in.

1.11 A. Vancouver's Pavel Bure

The Russian Rocket set an NHL record on February 28, 1998, when he wristed the puck past Ottawa Senators goalie Damian Rhodes to count his third penalty-shot goal of the season. Bure's other two penalty-shot markers came against the Coyotes' Nikolai Khabibulin on January 26, 1998, and the Sharks' Mike Vernon on November 12, 1997. The last player to have three penalty-shot attempts in a single season was Joe Mullen of the Calgary Flames in 1986-87. Mullen scored on all three shots, but one was disallowed because it was ruled that he had used an illegal stick.

1.12 D. 1987-88, Mario Lemieux

Gretzky won MVP honours nine out of 10 years during the 1980s, missing only in 1987-88, when Lemieux captured the Hart Trophy after winning the scoring race (168 points) and helping his last-place Penguins gain some measure of respectability.

1.13 C. Dave Andreychuk with Buffalo and Toronto

Only two NHLers have been traded midseason in their 50-goal year: Craig Simpson and Dave Andreychuk. Simpson was the first in 1987-88, when he posted a 56-goal season split between Pittsburgh (13 goals in 21 games) and Edmonton (43 goals in 59 games). But Andreychuk scored at least 25 goals with each team during his 50-goal trade year. After he had netted 29 goals for the Sabres in 52 games in 1992-93, Buffalo dealt Andreychuk to Toronto where he exploded for another 25 in his 31 remaining games for a career-high 54-goal season.

1.14 D. 10 teams

Michel Petit is the ultimate journeyman. He became the first player to suit up for a record 10 NHL teams in 1997-98. Petit's NHL pilgrimage included the Vancouver Canucks (1982-87), New York Rangers (1987-89), Quebec Nordiques (1990), Toronto Maple Leafs (1990-92), Calgary Flames (1992-94), Los Angeles Kings (1994-95), Tampa Bay Lightning (1995-96), Edmonton Oilers (1996), Philadelphia Flyers (1997) and the Phoenix Coyotes (1997-98). Since 1982, Petit has been drafted once, claimed on waivers once, signed as a free agent three times and been part of five trades involving 18 players. As of 1997-98, Petit's 10-team career leads all NHL journeymen, including one nine-team player (Brent Ashton), five eight-team players and 26 seven-team players.

NHL Players with Most Teams*

Player	Teams	TGP	PTS	Years	MPT*	GP
Michel Petit	10	827	328	15	Van	226
Brent Ashton	9	998	629	14	Wpg	222
Ken Hammond	8	193	47	8	LA	62
Larry Hillman	8	790	232	19	Tor	277
Walt McKechnie	8	955	606	16	Det	320
Dan Quinn	8	805	685	14	Pit	270
Rob Ramage	8	1,044	564	15	St.L	441

TGP/Total games played, MPT/Most prominent team, GP/Games played with most prominent team
* Current to 1997–98

1.15 B. Dale Hunter

Considering Hunter's penchant for the penalty box (almost 3,500 minutes as of 1997-98), it's remarkable he found the time to score 300 goals. To reach that milestone, Hunter, during his 18-plus years, has been a consistent 20-goal, 200 PIM player, amassing nine 20-goal seasons and 11 200-plus penalty-minute years. As of 1997-98, the feisty forward has had 100 or more PIM every year of his career.

1.16 A. Sergei Fedorov

Fedorov's nickname dates back to 1996-97, when the Detroit star complained about different standards between Russian players and those from North America, declaring things would be different "if my name were Sam Jones." During his lengthy contract impasse in 1997-98, some Detroit players were less than complimentary about Sam Jones. "Sam Jones is in Moscow now ... losing a lot of money," said Slava Kozlov. Based on his $5-million salary, Fedorov forfeited $25,000 a day during his holdout. As it turned out, that sum was pocket change to Fedorov, whose patience paid off when he signed hockey's most substantial contract to date, a $38-million deal with Detroit that included a $14-million signing bonus, $2 million in salary and another $12-million payment if the Wings reached the Western Conference finals.

1.17 C. Mario Lemieux

Lemieux's last regular-season goal was on a penalty shot. The milestone marker came in a 4-2 loss to the Florida Panthers on April 11, 1997. Ironically, it was also Lemieux's 50th goal of the season. His victim was John Vanbiesbrouck, the netminder Lemieux racked up the most goals against (30) in his career.

1.18 A. Three seconds

The Lemieux-McCarty feud was sparked by an incident in the 1996 playoffs when Lemieux's nasty blindside cross-check sent the Wings' Kris Draper to the hospital for reconstructive facial surgery. In retaliation for his teammate's injuries, McCarty bloodied Lemieux with a sucker punch in a brawl-filled game in Detroit in March 1997. Lemieux hardly defended himself, meekly turtling under McCarty's blows. In their next regular-season meeting, November 11, 1997, Lemieux switched his wing at the opening face-off so he could get closer to McCarty. Lemieux jawed with McCarty and the two squared off again, dropping their gloves just three seconds into the game. They fought toe-to-toe, Lemieux landing several rights and lefts to McCarty's face before the pair tumbled to the ice. "If you're going to do it, do it right off the bat," Lemieux said of the old score that needed settling. "Last year, the guys fought their hearts out for me. This was my payback for them." McCarty concluded: "He wanted to prove something to himself and his teammates. It was more or less his move. In my mind, he's still an idiot because he hasn't apologized to Drapes."

1.19 C. Six foot nine

Few NHLers stretch the tape beyond six foot six, but at six foot eight, 245 lbs., Los Angeles winger Steve McKenna is one of the biggest pro players in North America. Because of his gangly size, basketball was a natural for the Toronto native, but he stuck with hockey despite his (pardon the pun) shortcomings. "With my size, I've definitely got to work on my agility, skating and puckhandling," McKenna has said. Even bigger than McKenna is the Islanders' behemoth defenseman Zdeno Chara of the Czech Republic. At six foot nine, 255 lbs, Chara is the tallest player in NHL history. He was drafted 56th overall by New York in 1996.

1.20 D. Wayne Gretzky

The consummate playmaker, Gretzky routinely racked up 100-point seasons in less than 50 games. In 1983-84, he scored the NHL's fastest 100 points in just 34 games. The following year he did it in 35 games. Lemieux is the next fastest; he notched a 100-point season in 36 games in 1988-89. Between them, Gretzky and Lemieux have combined to record the 12 fastest 100-point years.

The NHL's Fastest 100-Point Players*			
Player	**Team**	**Season(s)**	**Game No.**
Wayne Gretzky	Edm	1983-84	34
Wayne Gretzky	Edm	1984-85	35
Mario Lemieux	Pit	1988-89	36
Wayne Gretzky	Edm	1981-82	38
Mario Lemieux	Pit	1992-93, 95-96	38
Wayne Gretzky	Edm	1985-86	39
Wayne Gretzky	Edm	1982-83, 86-87	42
Wayne Gretzky	Edm	1987-88	43
Mario Lemieux	Pit	1987-88	45
Wayne Gretzky	Edm	1988-89	47
Jari Kurri	Edm	1984-85	48
Bernie Nicholls	LA	1988-89	48

Current to 1997-98

1.21 C. Alexandre Daigle of the Ottawa Senators

After a stellar Canadian junior career with Victoriaville, where he was named the 1992 rookie of the year and selected to the QMJHL First All-Star Team in 1993, Daigle seemed the perfect fit for Ottawa. The Senators, with only 11 wins in their first season, needed an offensive star to sell tickets and help fill their new $185-million arena. Daigle's junior numbers were impressive and he was camera savvy in Canada's two official languages—a star-in-waiting capable of bridging both cultures in Canada's bilingual capital. The Senators were so hot on Daigle (considered the best French-Canadian junior since Mario Lemieux), some say they tanked a few games in 1992-93 to get the first pick. On the morning of the draft, Daigle was signed to an unprecedented five-year, $12.5-million deal. Unfortunately, the fairy tale went bust. The Senators got their new arena, but in 1998, after four more frustrating seasons, they traded their number one pick to Philadelphia. As one Ottawa headline declared: "He was the Can't Miss Kid, Who Did." Just after the trade, Flyer Chris Gratton, who went third in Daigle's draft, was asked if he had reminded his new team-mate of his 1993 comment, "Nobody remembers who was picked second." Gratton laughed: "Not yet, but I'm sure I'll bring it up once or twice, maybe when I get him in the corner during practice."

1.22 C. 1996-97
The NHL's last bareheaded player, Craig MacTavish of the Flyers, scored his last goal on November 9, 1996, against Calgary's Rick Tabaracci in a 3-2 win over the Flames. MacTavish played 50 games for St. Louis in 1996-97, his retirement year, picking up two goals and seven assists.

1.23 D. One mile above sea level
Denver, Colorado, is one mile (5,280 feet) above sea level. At that airy altitude, some visitors find they are breathing faster, heavier and deeper; they may also feel a shortness of breath when exercising. As the home-team Avalanche are more used to the effects of high altitude, it gives them a marginal advantage over visiting teams. As tiredness sets in more quickly because of the altitude, both home and visiting teams alike shorten their line changes, to about 30 to 40 seconds per shift.

1.24 D. Bill Clinton
The first sitting U.S. president to attend an NHL game was President Clinton, who watched the Washington Capitals defeat the Buffalo Sabres 3-2 on May 25, 1998, at Washington's

MCI Center. "It (hockey) is much more exciting in person, even, than on television—no offence to ESPN," Clinton said during the second period intermission. "I love this. It's fascinating." The American president sat in the luxury suite of Capitals owner Abe Poulin. Unfortunately, Clinton left the arena before Todd Krygier's overtime goal gave Washington a 3-2 victory.

1.25 D. Kenny Jonsson

Although the photograph contains a couple of clues, you've got to be a real Islanders fan to get this one. First, the season should be obvious from the 25th anniversary patch on the right shoulder: 1996-97. Second, no jersey name or number is identifiable, but part of a number appears above Fedorov's left glove. Could it be No. 3? Third, judging from the play, our mystery Islander must be taller than six foot one, Fedorov's height. Fourth, the player shoots left. Unfortunately, his name on the stick is blurred. Fifth, he wears Bauer pants and Cooper gloves and a helmet with a visor. Not much help since some players change equipment midseason. Who is he? At six foot three, shooting left, sporting a visor and wearing No.3 for the Islanders, it's Kenny Jonsson. The photo, by Bruce Bennett Studios of New York, was snapped December 28th, 1996, in a 7-1 loss to Detroit at Nassau Coliseum.

GAME 1
THE PUCK PUZZLE

In this game, each word joins in the same way as a regular crossword. Starting at square number one, work clockwise around the four concentric rings or toward the centre along the spokes, filling in the correct answer from the clues below. Each answer begins with the letter of the previous word. Determine word length by using the clue numbers (i.e., the answer to number one is nine letters long since the next clue is number three.)

(Solutions are on page 114)

Around

1. Montreal team
3. Dallas player
5. The "Richard _____"
6. Famous 1997 Russian goalie
8. Jerry _____, 15-year vet retired 1985
9. In alone on a goalie
12. Detroit's Steve _____
14. One-time NHL Quebec team
17. The Devils' Scott _____
21. Record or important math fact
21. Detroit's _____ Abel, retired 1954
22. Philly's Andre "Moose" _____
23. "Trash _____"
24. Habs and Avs Cup-winner Mike _____
25. Canes' Nelson _____
26. The "N" of NHL
27. Toronto team
28. "_____ a message"
29. Dick _____, 18-year vet, retired 1972
30. Mike _____, 15-year vet, retired 1994

31. One-time musical instrument in hockey arena, plural
32. Wilf _____, 14-year vet, retired 1988
33. _____ Horton
34. 1947 Rookie of the Year Howie _____
35. Old-time referee _____ Storey
36. The Leafs' Tie _____
37. Ted _____, 11-year vet, retired 1977
38. Nickname of Camille Henry
39. Title: _____ Stanley
40. _____ Hawerchuk
41. _____ van Impe
42. "_____ the puck in opponent's zone"
43. Red _____, 12-year vet, retired in 1940
44. "The team _____ to the occasion."
45. Brett is the _____ of Bobby
46. CBC's *Hockey _____ in Canada*
47. _____ Barrasso
48. Fan or _____ the puck
49. Isles goalie Billy _____

1. The Blackhawks' city
2. Nickname for player with most consecutive games played
4. Best player
7. New York team
8. Tom _____, 11-year vet, retired 1995
10. Habs old-timer Ken _____, retired 1950
11. "A _____ combination"
13. "Can't win them all," says coach, a _____
15. Canes' No. 28, Paul _____
16. Work; or "Their _____ paid off."
18. Brian _____, 11-year vet, retired 1987
20. 1997 Sens goalie, Ron _____

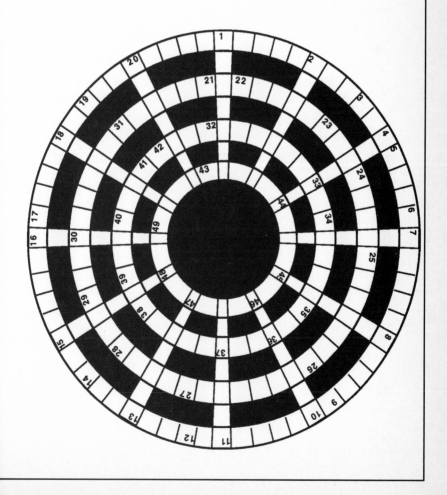

17

2

MARIO'S WORLD

When Mario Lemieux retired in 1997, he left behind a unique legacy. He was at first the stubborn draft choice, then later the hero of the 1987 Canada Cup and multiple Art Ross Trophy winner as the NHL's top scorer. Lemieux propelled the Pittsburgh Penguins from worst to first and two Stanley Cups; his goal scoring was electrifying, his battle with Hodgkin's disease a measure of his heart and courage. Lemieux's stardom saved the Pens' franchise and placed him on hallowed ground with baseball's Honus Wagner: the two greatest athletes in Pittsburgh sports history.

Perhaps his finest moment came in 1992. Despite missing six games to injuries, Lemieux led all playoff scorers with 16 goals and 34 points in 15 matches. He fired five game-winning goals enroute to the Cup and won the Conn Smythe Trophy as playoff MVP, prompting teammate Bryan Trottier to proclaim, "Right now, we're living in Mario's world."

(Answers are on page 22)

2.1 **When did Mario Lemieux begin wearing No.66?**
A. In 1978, in Pee Wee with the Ville Emard Hurricanes
B. In 1980, in Midget AAA with the Ville Emard Hurricanes
C. In 1981, in the QMJHL with the Laval Voisins
D. In 1984, in the NHL with the Pittsburgh Penguins

2.2 **Which All-Star defenseman did Mario Lemieux beat to score his first NHL goal?**
A. Boston's Ray Bourque
B. Montreal's Larry Robinson
C. Edmonton's Paul Coffey
D. Chicago's Chris Chelios

2.3 Considering Phil Esposito holds the NHL record for most shots on goal in one season (550 shots), what is the most shots on goal amassed by Mario Lemieux in one season?

A. Between 350 and 400 shots

B. Between 400 and 450 shots

C. Between 450 and 500 shots

D. Between 500 and 550 shots

2.4 When Mario Lemieux retired in 1997, where did he rank on the NHL's all-time goal scoring list?

A. Third place behind Wayne Gretzky and Gordie Howe

B. Fourth place

C. Fifth place

D. Sixth place

2.5 Mario Lemieux is the only NHLer to score a goal in every way in one game. How many different ways did Mario score?

A. Three different ways

B. Four different ways

C. Five different ways

D. Six different ways

2.6 Before Mario Lemieux arrived in Pittsburgh, the Penguins averaged 6,800 fans per game. How much did attendance increase during Lemieux's rookie year?

A. Attendance stayed the same in his rookie year

B. Between 1,000 and 2,500 fans

C. Between 2,500 and 4,000 fans

D. More than 4,000 fans

2.7 In 1988, Mario Lemieux won the Hart Trophy as league MVP while playing on a last-place team, the Pittsburgh Penguins. How many times in NHL history has a player won MVP status with a cellar dweller?

A. It has never happened

B. Two times

C. 10 times

D. 20 times

2.8 In what game did Mario Lemieux notch his 500th goal?
A. His 505th game
B. His 555th game
C. His 605th game
D. His 655th game

2.9 Wayne Gretzky's 47-point playoff total in 1985 is an NHL record. How many fewer points does Mario Lemieux have with the next-best league record?
A. One point less (46 points)
B. Three points less (44 points)
C. Five points less (42 points)
D. Seven points less (40 points)

2.10 Which player assisted on the most Mario Lemieux goals?
A. Kevin Stevens
B. Ron Francis
C. Paul Coffey
D. Jaromir Jagr

2.11 At the time of his retirement, which All-Star record did Mario Lemieux hold?
A. Most goals in one game
B. Most assists in one game
C. Most points in one game
D. Most power-play goals in one game

2.12 Which Canadian junior record did Mario Lemieux set in his final junior year in 1983-84?
A. Most goals in one season
B. Most points in one season
C. Longest consecutive game point-scoring streak
D. All of the above

2.13 When you compare the number of career goals scored by Mario Lemieux in his 745 games and Wayne Gretzky's goal count after 745 games, which statement is correct?
A. Gretzky scored three more goals
B. Gretzky scored 30 more goals
C. Lemieux scored three more goals
D. Lemeiux scored 30 more goals

2.14 When Mario Lemieux retired, he held the NHL record for highest goals-per-game average in a career. What was it?
A. Between .600 and .700 goals per game
B. Between .700 and .800 goals per game
C. Between .800 and .900 goals per game
D. More than .900 goals per game

2.15 How many games did Mario Lemieux miss after being diagnosed with cancer in 1992-93?
A. 23 games
B. 43 games
C. 63 games
D. 83 games

2.16 Out of a possible 1,020 games during his 13-year career, how many regular-season games did Mario Lemieux miss?
A. Between 100 and 200 games
B. Between 200 and 300 games
C. Between 300 and 400 games
D. More than 400 games

2.17 What was Mario Lemieux's longest point-scoring streak in the NHL?
A. 26 games
B. 36 games
C. 46 games
D. 56 games

2.18 How many NHL records did Mario Lemieux hold or share when he retired in 1997?
A. Five NHL records
B. 10 NHL records
C. 20 NHL records
D. 30 NHL records

MARIO'S WORLD
Answers

2.1 **C. In 1981, in the QMJHL with the Laval Voisins**
From the ages of seven to 15, Lemieux played for a local team called the Ville Emard Hurricanes in Mosquito, Atom, Pee Wee and Bantam division hockey. Usually, he wore No.27, his big brother Alain's number. Then, in 1981, before joining Laval in major junior hockey, his co-agent Bob Perno suggested trying another number, one that would make Lemieux distinct from his brother yet would also be a comparison to Wayne Gretzky. They flipped Wayne's No.99 around and Mario had his new sweater number, No.66. It was special; no other hockey player in the world was using it. Lemieux wore it first with the Laval Voisins in 1981-82, when he scored 30 goals and, appropriately enough, 66 assists.

2.2 **A. Boston's Ray Bourque**
Just 78 seconds after stepping onto the ice in his first NHL game, Lemieux scored his first professional goal. With the Bruins on the attack, Mario went to the point as Bourque was about to fire a shot. The blast hit Lemieux in the pads. He picked up the loose puck, shifted around the Boston All-Star and was gone for a clean breakaway on goalie Pete Peeters. Lemieux deked Peeters out of position with a brilliant move to pot his first NHL goal. It came in Mario's first game, on his first shift, on his first shot.

2.3 A. Between 350 and 400 shots

Lemieux recorded a career total of 3,054 shots in regular-season action, but his best single-season shot total came in 1987-88, when he fired a league-high 382 shots and scored 70 times. Interestingly, Lemieux's next two-highest shots-on-goal counts were during his two last seasons: 1995-96 (338 shots) and 1996-97 (327 shots).

2.4 D. Sixth place

Lemieux retired in sixth place (613 goals) among NHL goal leaders, in 11th position (881 assists) among league assist leaders and in sixth place (1,494 points) among point leaders.

2.5 C. Five different ways

On December 31, 1988, Lemieux conducted a clinic in goal scoring, recording goals in every conceivable fashion: at even strength on a pass from Rob Brown; shorthanded on a slap shot above the left face-off circle; on the power play with a shot that dribbled through New Jersey goalie Bob Sauve's legs; on a penalty shot against Chris Terreri, who had replaced Sauve; and into an empty net. It's the only time a player has scored in every manner possible in one game. The Penguins whipped the Devils 8-6.

2.6 C. Between 2,500 and 4,000 fans

Lemieux proved to be the consummate NHL franchise player. With the Penguins averaging less than 7,000 fans per game, Pittsburgh general manager Eddie Johnston disregarded his scout's advice (he liked Kirk Muller as top draft pick) and resisted the offers of other NHL teams who dangled attractive trade packages, and selected Lemieux first overall in 1984. "There's no question," Johnston said. "If we didn't take him (at the draft), the Civic Arena would be a parking lot now." The Penguins claim attendance jumped by 3,200 per game after Lemieux arrived. As well as keeping the team in Pittsburgh and helping to produce the championships that followed, Lemieux was responsible for influencing a generation of young players to try the game in new rinks that began popping up in Pennsylvania.

2.7   B. Two times
Since the Hart Trophy was first awarded in 1924, only three players have won MVP honours on last-place teams. In 1987-88, Lemieux did it by amassing a season-high 168 points, though his Penguins finished in the Patrick Division basement. But two other NHLers also share this "good news-bad news" oddity: MVP-winner Tom Anderson of the last-place Brooklyn Americans in 1941-42, and Hart Trophy-recipient Al Rollins, who backstopped the hapless Chicago Blackhawks to a disastrous 12-40-17 record in 1953-54. (Ironically, years later in 1976-77, when Rollins coached the WHA Phoenix Roadrunners to last place, his star player, Robbie Ftorek, won MVP honours.)

2.8   C. His 605th game
Lemieux scored his 500th career goal in his 605th game, quicker than anyone else in NHL history except Wayne Gretzky (575 games). The goal, which came on October 26, 1995, in a 7-5 win over the New York Islanders, capped a three-goal performance, his 32nd career hat trick.

2.9   B. Three points less (44 points)
If Wayne Gretzky set the standard by which Mario Lemieux is measured, then perhaps Lemieux's greatest scoring accomplishment is his 44-point playoff year in 1991, just three behind Gretzky's all-time record of 47 points. During the 23 games, Lemieux fired a playoff-high 93 shots, scored 16 times and assisted on 28 others. In the 1991 finals against Minnesota, his most important goal came in game two. With the Pens leading 2-1, he wheeled through centre ice, split Minnesota D-men Shawn Chambers and Neil Wilkinson with a deft move, then deked goalie Jon Casey and flipped a backhander between the posts as he was falling to the ice. From that moment on the Stars knew a healthy Lemieux was almost impossible to contain. For many, it was the play that turned the series.

2.10 C. Paul Coffey

Of the 110 players credited with assists on Lemieux's goals, no player has done more than Coffey, who helped Mario net 72 of his 613 regular-season markers. Jagr assisted on 68, Stevens on 64 and Francis on 60. Lemieux scored 53 goals unassisted.

2.11 C. Most points in one game

Lemieux became the first NHLer to score more than four points in an All-Star game on February 9, 1988, when he notched three goals and three assists to lead the Wales Conference to a 6-5 overtime win. After accounting for a point on every Wales goal scored in regulation time, Lemeiux popped the game winner at 1:08 of overtime. His awesome performance left few in doubt of his MVP status. Lemieux's six-point game is one point better than five other NHLers who share second place (five points) in this category. Mario is tied with three other players for most goals (four) in one All-Star game.

2.12 D. All of the above

Lemieux's third and final junior season established records still unbroken for most goals, most points and longest point-scoring streak. He shattered the previous Canadian junior mark of his idol Guy Lafleur by scoring 133 goals, broke Pierre Larouche's point total with 282 points and erased Doug Gilmour's record for the longest point-scoring streak by scoring in 61 straight games. To beat Gilmour in that category, Lemeiux decided not to represent Canada at the 1984 World Junior Hockey Championships in Europe, because it would mean missing games at home and the Christmas season with his family. Unpopular as the decision was, he held fast. He set the record and had a great family vacation. It was classic Lemieux. He did it his way, in his time. His junior totals in 1983-84 were a magical 133-149-282 in 70 games.

2.13 A. Gretzky scored three more goals

Mario finished his 745-game career with 613 goals, just three fewer than Gretzky, who scored 616 times during his first 745 games. Gretzky had a substantial lead with 1,774 points compared to Lemieux's 1,494.

2.14 C. Between .800 and .900 goals per game

Among players with 200 or more goals in their careers, Lemieux has the highest average of goals scored in regular-season games. Between 1984-85 and 1996-97, Mario's 613 goals in 745 games yielded .823 goals per game, the NHL's best scoring record and one that may never be broken. In playoff matches, Lemieux's average is .787 goals per game on 70 goals in 89 games.

The NHL's Highest Goals-Per-Game Averages*

Player	Team	Years	Goals	Games	Avg.
Mario Lemieux	Pit	1984-1997	613	745	.823
Cy Denneny	Ott/Bos	1917-1929	250	326	.767
Mike Bossy	NYI	1977-1987	573	752	.762
Brett Hull	Cal/St.L	1986-1997	527	735	.717
Wayne Gretzky	Edm/LA/				
	St.L/NYR	1979-1997	826	1,335	.646

*Based on year of Mario Lemieux's retirement, 1996-97

2.15 A. 23 games

Diagnosed with Hodgkin's disease after doctors removed an enlarged lymph node from his neck, Lemieux underwent seven weeks of radiation treatment, the last blast of radiation coming just 12 hours before his first game back on March 2, 1993. Lemieux played 21 minutes that night, netting a goal and an assist. "He's an amazing athlete," said winger Rich Tocchet in a *Pittsburgh Post-Gazette* story. The magnitude of his comeback was epic. He missed only 23 games to cancer, and on his return roared past Pat LaFontaine to win the NHL scoring race, with 69 goals and 160 points in just 60 games. After his comeback, he led the Penguins to 17 straight wins, an NHL record. Lemieux also claimed his second Hart Trophy as MVP and his first Masterton Trophy for perseverance and dedication.

2.16 B. Between 200 and 300 games

Lemieux missed 275 games during his career due to injuries and illness, the longest layoffs due to back surgeries in 1990 and

1993, and after his battle with cancer in 1993. He missed the entire 1994-95 season. Projected over 1,020 games, his .823 goals-per-game average would have yielded an 800-plus-goal career. "If I would have played more games and been healthy my whole career, maybe I would be up there with Gretzky," Lemieux said. "We'll never know, I guess."

2.17 C. 46 games
Lemieux scored an amazing 39 goals and 64 assists for 103 points during his longest consecutive point-scoring streak, 46 games in 1989-90. Playing with terrible back pain and "at less than 50 per cent," according to Lemieux, he couldn't even tie his own skates for the last 20 games of the streak. Finally, on February 14, he was forced to the sidelines. He played only 59 games but finished the season with 123 points, fourth best in the league. With a full slate of 80 games, Lemieux's two-points-per-game average would have earned him 160 points and another scoring title. During the off-season he underwent surgery to repair a herniated disk, a chronic problem during his career.

2.18 A. Five NHL records
Despite his superstar status, Lemieux left the game holding only five NHL records. He won all of the game's most important individual and team awards, including multiple Stanley Cups and Conn Smythe Trophies as playoff MVP, but the scoring records went to Wayne Gretzky, who was fortunate enough to play on superior teams early in his career. At the time of his retirement, Lemieux led the record books in five categories: most shorthanded goals in one season (13); most overtime goals in a career (9); most overtime points in a career (19); highest goals-per-game average in a career (.823); and most goals in one period (four—shared with 10 others).

GAME 2
SNIPERS OF 1992-93

No NHL season has produced more 100-point players than 1992-93. A total of 21 marksmen hit the century mark, but only one player did it before 1992 was over. In fact, that player and Wayne Gretzky are the only two players in NHL history to score their 100th point of the season before the start of the new year.

In this game, 20 of the 21 players listed below appear in the puzzle horizontally, vertically or backwards. Some are easily found, such as TEEMU, written backwards; others require a more careful search. After you've circled all 39 *first* and *last* names, read the remaining 12 letters in descending order to spell the name of the only player of 1992-93 to score his 100th point before the start of 1993.

To get started, here is a list of the first names that need to be circled; you fill in the last names and circle them too. (There are two players named Joe, but look for only one "Joe" in the puzzle; both last names are there.)

(Solutions are on page 115)

Pat _____	Adam _____
Steve _____	Pierre _____
Doug _____	Alexander _____
Mark _____	Teemu _____
Luc _____	Kevin _____
Mats _____	Pavel _____
Jeremy _____	Craig _____
Rick _____	Joe _____
Ron _____	Brett _____
Theoren _____	Joe _____

```
M S N E V E T S I C N A R F
N E R O E H T E H C C O T L
I B U R E R R E I P B A U D
V R N O R U O M L I G C I O
E (U M E E T) O A T E S O L U
K B Y Z E R M A N E M I L G
R R E C C H I I A D A M L I
A E S S E L A N N E E U U A
M T T X L T U R G E O N H R
P T A E N I D N U S A K I C
A A M O G I L N Y E N N A J
V P F L E U R Y M E R E J O
E A L E X A N D E R I C K E
L K C I N E O R J U N E A U
```

3

NO. 99, THE GRIND LINE AND HOCKEY'S MOST FAMOUS PUCK

Did Wayne Gretzky ever wear a sweater number other than No.99? Which forward lines were named because of their defensive work or their abrasive style? And what ever happened to the puck that won the 1972 Summit Series for Canada? In this chapter we check out some unusual hockey stories on sweater numbers, nicknames for less-than-familiar trios and hockey's most famous puck.

(Answers are on page 34)

3.1 Besides No.99, what is the only other jersey number worn by Wayne Gretzky in his pro career?
A. No.9
B. No.10
C. No.20
D. No.79

3.2 Which three-time Stanley Cup-winning Montreal Canadien was the last Boston player to wear No.4 before it was given to Bobby Orr?
A. Al Langlois
B. Reggie Fleming
C. Andre Pronovost
D. Marcel Bonin

3.3 What name was given to Philadelphia's line of centre Daniel Lacroix and wingers Dan Kordic and Brantt Myhres in 1997-98?
A. The Sin Bin Line
B. The Bus Line
C. The KLM Line
D. The Left Hook Line

3.4 As of 1997-98, how many U.S.-born players have had their jersey numbers retired by NHL teams?
A. One American player
B. Two American players
C. Four American players
D. Eight American players

3.5 Prior to 1997-98, when Mark Messier wore No.11, when was the last time that a Vancouver Canucks player wore No.11? (Name the player, if any.)
A. 1972-73
B. 1982-83
C. 1992-93
D. No Canuck had ever worn No.11 before Mark Messier

3.6 Name the only Chicago Blackhawk to wear No.9 after Bobby Hull signed with the WHA in 1972?
A. Pit Martin
B. Dennis Hull
C. Dale Tallon
D. Keith Magnuson

3.7 What was the sweater size of the Red Wings jersey that decorated the Spirit of Detroit statue during the Wings-Flyers Stanley Cup finals in 1997?
A. Size 60
B. Size 160
C. Size 260
D. Size 360

3.8 Which 1997-98 team featured The Grind Line?
A. The New York Rangers
B. The Detroit Red Wings
C. The Phoenix Coyotes
D. The Vancouver Canucks

3.9 Which team banned the wearing of high sweater numbers in 1997-98?
A. The Calgary Flames
B. The Tampa Bay Lightning
C. The Ottawa Senators
D. The Anaheim Mighty Ducks

3.10 After wearing No.96 for two seasons, which jersey number did Vancouver's Pavel Bure switch back to in 1997-98?
A. No.9
B. No.10
C. No.16
D. No.22

3.11 What WHA player had his number retired by an NHL team, even though he never played for that club in the NHL?
A. Winnipeg's Bobby Hull
B. Hartford's Gordie Howe
C. Edmonton's Al Hamilton
D. Quebec's J. C. Tremblay

3.12 The LCB Line played for which Stanley Cup-winning team during the 1970s?
A. The Boston Bruins
B. The Philadelphia Flyers
C. The Montreal Canadiens
D. The New York Islanders

3.13 What word did Dallas Star defenseman Darryl Sydor stitch on his jersey in 1997-98?
A. Mom
B. Defense
C. Courage
D. Peace

3.14 Which well-known NHLers were Mark Messier's linemates in
the WHA's final season?
A. Wayne Gretzky and Frank Mahovlich
B. Ulf Nilsson and Anders Hedberg
C. Mike Gartner and Robbie Ftorek
D. Gordie Howe and Mark Howe

3.15 Which NHL team first experimented with long pants for their
uniforms?
A. The New York Islanders
B. The Chicago Blackhawks
C. The Hartford Whalers
D. The Philadelphia Flyers

3.16 As of 1997-98, how many European-trained players have had
their numbers retired?
A. One European player
B. Two European players
C. Four European players
D. Six European players

3.17 What was the name of the Winnipeg Jets line that Bobby
Hull, Anders Hedberg and Ulf Nilsson played on?
A. The Golden Jet Line
B. The Hot Line
C. The International Line
D. The Swedish Express

3.18 Who has the puck that Paul Henderson used to score the
winning goal in the 1972 Canada-Russia Summit Series?
A. The Hockey Hall of Fame
B. Team Canada member Paul Henderson
C. A Soviet Ice Hockey Federation official
D. A Team Canada member other than Paul Henderson

NO. 99, THE GRIND LINE AND HOCKEY'S MOST FAMOUS PUCK
Answers

3.1 C. No.20
Gretzky has worn only one other sweater besides No.99 during his entire pro career. It happened on November 3, 1978, in his first WHA game as an Edmonton Oiler. The Oilers didn't have a jersey bearing his famous No.99 ready, so Gretzky was handed No.20. The number switch had little adverse effect; Gretzky scored his first Oiler goal in the club's 4-3 win over Winnipeg. In the next game, Gretzky donned his traditional double nines.

3.2 A. Al Langlois
Nicknamed "Junior," Langlois won Cups with Montreal in 1958, 1959 and 1960 before being traded to New York, Detroit and Boston—where in 1965-66 he played his last NHL season wearing the Bruins' No.4. The following year No.4 was handed to Orr, who made it his own forever.

3.3 D. The Left Hook Line
Lines are usually named for their scoring prowess. In Philadelphia, where hockey is a serious passion, even a checking line of tough guys gets christened. Lacroix, Kordic and Myhres combined for only two goals and seven points in 1997-98, but their penalty totals of 135, 210 and 169 minutes reflect the gritty moniker, The Left Hook Line.

3.4 B. Two American players
Among the 70 NHLers with retired numbers in 1997-98, only two U.S.-born players have been so distinguished: Rod Langway and Neal Broten. Langway, two-time Norris Trophy-winner (1983 and 1984) as the league's best defenseman, was honoured on November 26, 1997, when his No.5 was raised to the rafters by Washington during the Capitals' last game at USAir Arena. The opponent that night was the Montreal Canadiens, the only other NHL team for which Langway

played. His trade from Montreal to the Caps in 1983 signaled new beginnings for Washington, which had suffered eight long years as the NHL's doormat. Neal Broten's No.7 was retired by the Dallas Stars on February 7, 1998. In 16 seasons with the Minnesota North Stars and Dallas Stars, Broten recorded 274 goals and 593 assists in 992 games.

3.5 A. 1972-73

The last Canuck to wear No.11 before Messier was Wayne Maki, who joined Vancouver in its inaugural season (1970-71) and played with the club for three years before his untimely death from cancer in 1974. Afterwards, the number was "unofficially" retired and Vancouver's media guide listed No.11 as "no longer worn." But when Messier signed with the Canucks in 1997, he took his longtime playing number, much to the dismay of Maki's widow, Beverly Maki. She wanted an acknowledgement that the number was retired and assurance that when Messier moved on No.11 would be re-retired. The team offered to mount a plaque at GM Place in Maki's honour.

3.6 C. Dale Tallon

There was such bitterness in the Blackhawks' front office after Hull defected to the NHL that they had his team stats temporarily erased and his famous jersey No.9 assigned to defenseman Dale Tallon. Tallon used No.9 for a week before handing it back, calling it "sacrilege" for anyone but Hull to wear it.

3.7 D. Size 360

To cheer on the Red Wings during their 1997 Stanley Cup run, employees of East Side Team Sports in Warren, Michigan, dressed the muscular shoulders of the Spirit of Detroit statue in a giant Detroit jersey. The statue, outside the City County building, required a size 360. It's probably the largest hockey sweater ever made.

3.8 B. The Detroit Red Wings

Detroit coach Scotty Bowman has put together some great scoring lines in his time, but few have been as successful at *not* scoring as his combination of Kris Draper, Kirk Maltby and Joe Kocur. Better known as The Grind Line, the trio specializes in grinding down first-line opponents along the boards.

3.9   C.   The Ottawa Senators
In September 1997, Ottawa general manager Pierre Gauthier ordered all his players with high jersey numbers to switch to numbers below 35. That left five players looking for new digits on their backs. Alexandre Daigle was forced to give up his familiar No.91 in favor of No.9; Radek Bonk switched from No.76 to 14; Stan Neckar from No.94 to 24; Denny Lambert from No.42 to 28 and Radim Bicanek from No.44 to 23. Gauthier said the move was taken to promote team unity. "To me big numbers singled out people from the rest of the team," Gauthier said. "This is a team sport and I think sometimes we forget that."

3.10 B. No.10
The Russian Rocket switched from No.96 back to No.10, the number he wore in his first four NHL seasons when he scored 174 goals. Prompted by the urge to acquire a unique number for himself, Bure changed to No.96 in 1995-96. With his new number, Bure staggered through two injury-plagued seasons, scoring just 29 goals in 78 games. After returning to No.10 in 1997-98, the Canucks superstar rebounded with a 51-goal year. "I had more luck with No.10," Bure said. If Bure wasn't superstitious before, you can bet he is now.

3.11 D. Quebec's J. C. Tremblay
Perhaps the most honoured tradition a player can receive from his team is having his sweater number retired. When the WHA folded in 1979, players such as J. C. Tremblay of Quebec and Hartford's John McKenzie retired after many years of WHA and NHL service. Although neither Tremblay (No.3) nor McKenzie (No.19) ever played an NHL game as a Quebec Nordique or Hartford Whaler, both had their numbers retired by the NHL clubs. In the case of Hull, Howe and Hamilton, each played for the NHL teams that retired their numbers.

3.12 B. The Philadelphia Flyers

Not all of those brawling Flyers from the 1970s were Broad Street Bullies. Philadelphia's two consecutive Stanley Cups (1974 and 1975) were won not only by intimidation through thuggery, but also by great goaltending from Bernie Parent, the offense of 50-goal scorer Rick MacLeish and the LCB Line of Reggie Leach, Bobby Clarke and Bill Barber. From day one the threesome clicked. Clarke, the gritty centre, was the line's workhorse and sparkplug; Barber and Leach were its tenacious scoring wingers. They came together by design, the handy work of Flyer general manager Keith Allen, who in 1974 picked up Leach from California and then, three days later, sent Bill Flett (the line's original right wing) to Toronto. The move was a natural considering Leach and Clarke's junior days in Flin Flon, Manitoba. "I knew of their great success together, so I wanted to see if they could do it again here," Allen recalls. The combo clicked and in 1975-76 they scored 141 goals. No Flyer line, including the Legion of Doom, has topped that incredible season. The LCB Line played together for nine years.

3.13 A. Mom

Since NHL rules don't permit personal patches on the outside of jerseys, Sydor stitched one word—Mom—on the inside of his sweater, a tribute to his mother, Anne Sydor, who died October 19, 1997. Anne, 55, suffered a heart attack in Edmonton. Her last night was spent watching her son on CBC's "Hockey Night in Canada," as Dallas defeated Toronto, 5-4.

3.14 C. Mike Gartner and Robbie Ftorek

Messier has always considered the WHA a "great stepping stone" to his career in the NHL. He jumped from Tier II hockey to the Cincinnati Stingers in 1978-79, where he scored only one goal on a line with Gartner and Ftorek. Gartner, also a rookie, scored 27 times that season, while Ftorek had 39 markers to help earn him 116 points and a second-place finish in the WHA scoring race. Messier's lone goal was a puck dump that wound up in the net. As Messier recalls, "You can see why I didn't help Robbie Ftorek win the scoring title that season."

3.15 D. The Philadelphia Flyers

In the early 1980s, some hockey manufacturers began designing uniforms that replaced traditional short pants and stockings with a heavily padded girdle and long, shell pants that extended from the waist to the skates. The Flyers, and later the Whalers, both experimented with long pants but, after much criticism, returned to the usual hockey uniform.

3.16 A. One European player

Although Chicago's Stan Mikita (No.21) and Bob Nystrom (No.23) of the New York Islanders have had their numbers retired, neither Mikita nor Nystrom were trained in their native countries of Czechoslovakia and Sweden. Both came to Canada at early ages. As of 1997-98, the only European-trained player with a retired NHL number is Sweden's Thomas Steen. Steen played 14 seasons, all in Winnipeg, scoring 264 goals and 817 points between 1981 and 1995. He holds team records in seasons played, most games (950) and career assists (553) for Phoenix/Winnipeg. Upon his retirement, Steen's No.25 jersey was hung from the rafters in Winnipeg Arena.

3.17 B. The Hot Line

What the name lacked in originality, the line made up in on-ice performance, becoming the most explosive scoring force in the WHA. Regardless of their position on the ice, each linemate somehow knew where the other was going to be. According to Anders Hedberg in *WHA—Same Game, Different Name*, "We never really had plays or planned where to move. We could interchange positions. It was a style Bobby always wanted to play." In its first season, 1974-75, the Hot Line combined for an amazing 362 points, as Hull scored 50 goals in 50 games to tie Maurice Richard's historic 50-in-50 record and then, later that year, eclipsed the 76-goal mark of Phil Esposito. Hull amassed 142 points, Nilsson counted 120 points (including 94 assists) and Hedberg earned 53 goals and 100 points. Nilsson once said: "I may have had the toughest role on that line because Bobby and Anders both wanted to score goals. Bobby yelled at me if I passed the puck to Anders. I heard the same, only in Swedish, from Anders, if I gave the puck to Hull. When I took a shot on goal, I got an earful from both of them."

3.18 D. A Team Canada member other than Paul Henderson
For many Canadians, Henderson's 1972 Summit Series goal stands as hockey's greatest moment. The Canada-Soviet Union hockey series was the first encounter between hockey's two superpowers. It was Canada defending its national sport, indeed its pride, and as 15 million of Canada's 20 million people looked on, Henderson scored in the dying seconds of the final game in Moscow. He was mobbed by the entire team after the goal, but whatever happened to the puck? The speculation ended in 1997 when Team Canada defenseman Pat Stapleton revealed its whereabouts in a story published in *The Globe and Mail*. As his teammates were celebrating Henderson's goal, Stapleton scooped up the puck. "The truth is, it's in a box with a lot of other pucks," he told reporter David Shoalts. "It was stored away about 20 years ago, and it's still there." But Stapleton, who made a habit out of saving pucks from important games, is able to identify it. "It's just plain black, but it's marked." Rather than sell it or donate it to the Hockey Hall of Fame, Stapleton plans to return it to the game's roots. "What I want to do is skate with it with my grandchildren on the pond. What we'll do is skate around for a while and then shoot it into a snowbank. And that'll be it."

GAME 3
TERRIFIC TRIOS

Few teams in the 1980s and 1990s have found the ideal player combinations to form potent threesomes. Philadelphia's Legion of Doom was an exception, at least until the Flyers traded Mikael Renberg in 1997, breaking up the trio for good. Since the trade, Doomers Eric Lindros and John LeClair have been matched with a number of Flyer forwards, an expected move considering that two-man units with a third man in rotation have become the recent norm. At one time, NHL teams kept their scoring lines together for years, even decades. In this game, match the teams below with the famous lines they iced.

(Solutions are on page 116)

1. ____ Toronto Maple Leafs
2. ____ Boston Bruins
3. ____ Montreal Maroons
4. ____ New York Islanders
5. ____ Detroit Red Wings
6. ____ Los Angeles Kings
7. ____ Buffalo Sabres
8. ____ Vancouver Canucks
9. ____ Philadelphia Flyers
10. ____ New York Rangers
11. ____ Chicago Blackhawks
12. ____ Montreal Canadiens

A. The Legion of Doom
B. The Triple Crown Line
C. The Production Line
D. The Scooter Line
E. The Long Island Lighting Co.
F. The Kid Line
G. The French Connection
H. The Nitro Line
I. The GAG Line
J. The S Line
K. The Punch Line
L. The Life Line

4

THE WHA: RENEGADE LEAGUE

No other professional league ever challenged the NHL like the World Hockey Association. From its inception in 1972 the WHA created new jobs, increased salaries and brought the game to places that had never seen hockey before.

In this chapter we look at seven seasons of the weird, wonderful and wacky from a renegade league that gave Gordie Howe a chance to play with his sons, brought us the first European snipers—along with rookies such as Wayne Gretzky and Mark Messier—and caused the greatest expansion hockey has ever known.

(Answers are on page 45)

4.1 **Who was the very first NHL defector to the WHA?**
   A. A player
   B. A coach
   C. A general manager
   D. A referee

4.2 **Who was the first NHL player to sign a WHA contract?**
   A. Derek Sanderson
   B. Wayne Connelly
   C. Bernie Parent
   D. Bobby Hull

4.3 **What was Bobby Hull's WHA contract with the Winnipeg Jets worth?**
   A. $1.75 million over 10 years
   B. $2.75 million over 10 years
   C. $3.75 million over 10 years
   D. $4.75 million over 10 years

4.4 How many teams were in the NHL when the WHA began operations in 1972?
A. 12 teams
B. 14 teams
C. 16 teams
D. 17 teams

4.5 What hockey first did Cincinnati Stingers Robbie Ftorek and teammate Claude Larose accomplish in the WHA?
A. They each recorded two penalty shots in one game
B. They each assisted on Wayne Gretzky's first pro goal
C. They each wore the same jersey number for the Stingers
D. They each share credit for scoring the first goal Stinger history

4.6 Who were the "Baby Bulls" of the WHA?
A. A rookie scoring line in New York
B. Underage juniors signed by Birmingham
C. A defensive duo in Edmonton
D. A trio of 300-plus penalty-minute fighters with Minnesota

4.7 In his rookie WHA season, which future NHL All-Star was speared by Gordie Howe after he beat up Marty Howe?
A. Mark Howe
B. Wayne Gretzky
C. Mike Gartner
D. Michel Goulet

4.8 Which NHLer is the only player in WHA history to lead (or share the lead) the WHA in goals, assists and points in one season?
A. Marc Tardif
B. Robbie Ftorek
C. Bobby Hull
D. Wayne Gretzky

4.9 How many games did NHL great Derek Sanderson play in the WHA?
   A. None
   B. Eight games
   C. 48 games
   D. One season

4.10 What was the name of the WHA's championship trophy?
   A. The WHA World Cup
   B. The Avco World Trophy
   C. The International Championship Trophy
   D. The Murphy Bowl

4.11 Who is the only bench boss to win coach of the year honours in both the WHA and the NHL?
   A. Bill Dineen
   B. Jacques Demers
   C. John Brophy
   D. Bobby Kromm

4.12 How many NHL cities played host to WHA franchises?
   A. Three NHL cities
   B. Five NHL cities
   C. Seven NHL cities
   D. Nine NHL cities

4.13 Who was called the "Bobby Orr" of the WHA after he became only the second defenseman in pro hockey to lead his team in scoring?
   A. Chicago's Pat Stapleton
   B. Winnipeg's Lars-Erik Sjoberg
   C. Quebec's J. C. Tremblay
   D. New England's Rick Ley

4.14 Besides Bobby Hull, who is the only other player to score 50 goals in both the NHL and the WHA?
A. Rick Vaive
B. Blaine Stoughton
C. Michel Goulet
D. Wayne Gretzky

4.15 How much did the WHA Edmonton Oilers pay to acquire the rights to Wayne Gretzky in 1978?
A. Less than $1 million
B. $1 million
C. $2 million
D. $3 million

4.16 What future NHL bench boss coached the most games in WHA history?
A. Jacques Demers
B. Glen Sather
C. Bill Dineen
D. Harry Neale

4.17 After the NHL-WHA merger in 1979, how many former WHA players were chosen in the first round (among 21 draft selections) of the 1979 NHL Entry Draft?
A. One WHA player, Mike Gartner
B. Three WHA players
C. Five WHA players
D. No WHA players were selected in the first round

4.18 Based on championships and final playoff-round appearances, which WHA team can be considered the league's most dominant powerhouse?
A. The Houston Aeros
B. The New England Whalers
C. The Quebec Nordiques
D. The Winnipeg Jets

4.19 Which future NHL coach was the first American to score more than 100 points in a season in pro hockey?
A. Robbie Ftorek
B. Herbert Brooks
C. Ron Wilson
D. Craig Patrick

4.20 As of 1997-98, how many WHA players were still playing in the NHL?
A. Two players
B. Three players
C. Four players
D. Five players

THE WHA: RENEGADE LEAGUE
Answers

4.1 **D. A referee**
On January 7, 1972, long-time NHL official Vern Buffey became the first NHL turncoat to sign a contract with the WHA. A month later, in his new position as referee-in-chief, Buffey supervised the new league's inaugural player draft, as 1,081 amateur and pro players were selected from around the world.

4.2 **C. Bernie Parent**
Two weeks after the WHA's inaugural player draft, the Miami Screaming Eagles announced the signing of Toronto Maple Leafs goalie Bernie Parent to a long-term deal for $750,000. The outlaw league had landed its first "name" player. "At my present salary, it would take me 10 to 15 years to make the kind of money I'm going to make in Miami," said Parent. But the Eagles folded before playing a game and Parent found himself backstopping their successors, the Philadelphia Blazers. After one WHA season, he crossed town to begin his Hall of Fame career with the Flyers. After Parent jumped to the WHA, Wayne Connelly signed a WHA contract, also in early 1972. The Parent and Connelly deals happened months before the

Bobby Hull signing, which sparked an explosion of NHL defections, including established stars such as Gerry Cheevers, Ted Green and J. C. Tremblay.

4.3 A. $1.75 million over 10 years
Hull's 10-year contract worked this way: For the first five years the Golden Jet received $250,000 annually as player-coach. The final five years he got a stipend of $100,000 per annum. His signing bonus was an unprecedented $1 million. For the upstart league it was a bargain, considering Hull's value at the box office. Meanwhile, the Blackhawks were only offering their multiple 50-goal scorer $100,000 per season. Frustrated by the impasse in negotiations with the Hawks, Hull tried to use the WHA as a bargaining ploy. As he recalled in *Sports Illustrated*, "I thought it (the WHA offer) was a joke. I pretended to go along with it, just to scare Chicago. Then my agent, Harvey Weinberg, said, 'Bobby, these guys are serious.'" Hull's signing gave the WHA instant credibility, and as Winnipeg general manager Annis Stukus said, "Bobby made us major league."

4.4 C. 16 teams
The NHL had no plans to increase its membership until 1974-75, but with the pending arrival of the WHA, the NHL Board of Governors reassessed its position and decided "it is in the best business interests to expand now." It was no coincidence that the NHL expanded to 16 teams, admitting the Atlanta Flames and the New York Islanders at the start of the 1972-73 season, the same year the WHA began operations.

4.5 C. They each wore the same jersey number for the Stingers
Both Ftorek and Larose had good reason for wanting sweater No.8 in Cincinnati. Larose had enjoyed a successful NHL career with No.8, and Ftorek had worn the number his entire pro career as a tribute to ex-Bruin Fleming Mackell. In an unprecedented move, Cincinnati received special permission from the league so that both players could wear the Stingers' No.8 during 1977-78.

4.6   B. Underage juniors signed by Birmingham

When Birmingham Bulls owner John Bassett broke the league's "gentleman's agreement" against signing underage juniors by inking 18-year-old Ken Linseman to a contract, it opened the door to other junior signings, including Indianapolis Racers owner Nelson Skalbania's deal with 17-year-old scoring ace Wayne Gretzky. In response, Bassett signed teenagers Rick Vaive, Craig Hartsburg, Gaston Gingras and Rob Ramage. They became known as Birmingham's "Baby Bulls."

4.7   D. Michel Goulet

Gordie and his sons Mark and Marty played together seven seasons: six in the WHA after signing in unison with Houston in 1973-74, and one as NHL Whalers in 1979-80. A favourite story involves rookie Michel Goulet, who took on Marty Howe in a fight one night. Goulet won against the younger Howe, but after the penalties were served, Goulet faced Gordie in the face-off circle. "What I remember next was clutching my stomach. Gordie had speared me and yelled into my ear 'Never touch my son.'" Blood is thicker than water, even on ice. The Howes' first pro goal together came on November 18, 1973, when Mark scored on assists by Gordie and Marty in an 8-3 Houston loss to the Quebec Nordiques.

4.8   A. Marc Tardif

After four seasons and two Stanley Cups with the Montreal Canadiens in the 1970s, Tardif moved to the WHA where he won two league scoring titles with Quebec. During the WHA's brief history (1972 to 1979), three scoring leaders—Tardif, Andre LaCroix and Réal Cloutier—each won the title twice. But Tardif alone led the league in goals, assists and points. The Nordiques' speedy left-winger did it in 1975-76 (71-77-148) and again in 1977-78 (69-85-154). On both occasions Tardif's season-leading stats are asterisked, as he tied J. C. Tremblay (1975-76) and Ulf Nilsson (1977-78) for most assists.

4.9 B. Eight games

After Bobby Hull, the WHA's next highest-profile signing was Derek Sanderson, former NHL rookie of the year (1968) and two-time Stanley Cup winner with Boston. At the top of his game, Sanderson left the Bruins and signed a 10-year $2.35-million contract with the Philadelphia Blazers. But after just eight games and six points, Sanderson begged for his WHA release and the Blazers bought out the flamboyant centre's contract for a reported $1 million. Turk headed back to the Bruins but he never again hit the heights of his glory days, playing for five NHL teams during his last six seasons.

4.10 B. The Avco World Trophy

Commissioned and sponsored by Avco Financial Services as the symbol of team supremacy in the WHA, the $13,000 trophy suffered its share of indignities during its seven-year stint in the hockey spotlight. At the first league championships, the trophy wasn't finished on time for the live television on-ice presentation, so a substitute was hastily purchased at a Boston sporting goods store. Unfortunately, CBS cut away from the game early and the ceremony was never aired. Over the years, duplicates of the trophy were made for various reasons and, today, the Avco World Trophy has three homes. One trophy sits in Toronto at the Hockey Hall of Fame; another is on display at Winnipeg Arena, home of the last WHA champions; and the third resides in the Nova Scotia Sports Hall of Fame in Halifax.

4.11 D. Bobby Kromm

Kromm took coach of the year honours, guiding the WHA Winnipeg Jets to the Avco Trophy in 1975-76, before moving to the Detroit Red Wings, where he copped his second coaching trophy, the NHL's Jack Adams Award, in 1977-78. Kromm's "think defense" team strategy worked well in both leagues. Although the Jets possessed great firepower built around finesse players such as Bobby Hull, Kromm stressed "teams that usually give up the fewest goals usually claim first place more often than teams that score the most goals." He whittled the Jets' goals-against numbers down from 293 to 254 goals in 1974-75, their championship year. Then, in Detroit, Kromm took a cellar dweller to second place in the Norris Division, again reducing the goals-against from 309 to 266 goals in 1977-78, the year he won the Jack Adams Award.

4.12 C. Seven NHL cities
The Los Angeles Sharks, Chicago Cougars, New York Raiders, Vancouver Blazers, Toronto Toros, Philadelphia Blazers and Minnesota Fighting Saints each competed head-to-head for the public's hockey dollar against their NHL counterparts. None ever outdrew the NHL teams, with Minnesota surviving the longest among the seven, playing 335 regular-season games.

4.13 C. Quebec's J. C. Tremblay
Like Bobby Orr in 1969-70, when he led the Boston Bruins in point totals (33-87-120), Tremblay established himself as Quebec's defensive mainstay in 1972-73, notching a team-high 89 points to become only the second rearguard in history to capture his team's scoring title. Tremblay also led the WHA that season with 75 assists.

4.14 B. Blaine Stoughton
Besides Hull, who had five 50-goal NHL seasons and four 50-goal years in the WHA, Stoughton is the only other sniper to record 50-goal seasons in both the NHL and WHA. Stoughton blasted 52 goals with Cincinnati in 1976-77, and twice hit 50 in the NHL (including a league-leading 56 in 1979-80 with Hartford).

4.15 A. Less than $1 million
In 1978, after just eight games and six points as an Indianapolis Racer, 17-year-old rookie Wayne Gretzky (as well as Peter Driscoll and Eddie Mio) were sold for $850,000 by Racers owner Nelson Skalbania to Peter Pocklington of the Oilers. Skalbania had originally signed Gretzky to a personal-services contract, but after losing $40,000 a game in Indianapolis, he severed his ties with the teenager. The rest is history.

49

4.16 C. Bill Dineen

Dineen, with a record 554 WHA games (322-204-28), was the only bench boss to coach in every WHA season, guiding Houston from 1972-73 to 1977-78 and New England in 1978-79. Dineen also holds the distinction of being the only WHA coach to win two Avco Cups (Houston 1974, 1975). Later, in 1991, he became the head coach of the Philadelphia Flyers.

4.17 C. Five WHA players

Ten players from the WHA were chosen in the 1979 NHL Entry Draft, including five in the first round. Seven of the 10 draftees came from the Birmingham Bulls, a team with huge potential. Overall, NHL scouts had a relatively accurate bead on the talent. Quality players such as Rob Ramage, Mike Gartner and Michel Goulet went in the first round, but young Mark Messier was selected 48th overall. Wayne Gretzky was never drafted, since he had signed an extended personal-services contract with Edmonton owner Peter Pocklington.

WHA Players Selected in the 1979 NHL Draft

Draft Round	Previous WHA Team	Drafted by NHL Team
First Round		
1. Rob Ramage	Birmingham	Colorado
4. Mike Gartner	Cincinnati	Washington
5. Rick Vaive	Birmingham	Vancouver
6. Craig Hartsburg	Birmingham	Minnesota
20. Michel Goulet	Birmingham	Quebec
Second Round		
27. Gaston Gingras	Birmingham	Montreal
28. Pat Riggin	Birmingham	Atlanta
Third Round		
48. Mark Messier	Cincinnati	Edmonton
49. Keith Crowder	Birmingham	Boston
Fourth Round		
71. John Gibson	Winnipeg	Los Angeles

4.18 D. The Winnipeg Jets

The Jets list a number of accomplishments in North American pro hockey. Most important, Winnipeg's signing of NHL superstar Bobby Hull affected salary scales and player development. The team also instigated and fostered the introduction of Europeans to North American play. As a result, in its seven seasons in the WHA, Winnipeg appeared in the finals five times and won the Avco World Trophy on three occasions.

4.19 A. Robbie Ftorek

Before graduating to the NHL, Robbie Ftorek of Needham, Massachusetts, was a bona fide star in the WHA. In 1976-77, he finished fourth in league scoring with a 46-71-117 record and earned MVP status, one of the first Americans in pro hockey to do so. Although the WHA standard of hockey was a level below the NHL calibre of play, Ftorek did make it in the NHL, but he never again achieved similar offensive numbers once the two leagues merged. During his five WHA seasons, Ftorek chalked up an impressive four consecutive 100-point seasons in Phoenix and Cincinnati. His first century mark in 1975-76 was the first 100-point season for a U.S.-born player in pro hockey.

4.20 B. Three players

In 1997-98, only three WHA alumni remained in the NHL. Wayne Gretzky, Mark Messier and Mike Gartner all played their rookie seasons in the WHA.

GAME 4

NHL DEFECTORS

A number of prominent NHLers either began or concluded their hockey career in the WHA. In Part 1, match the well-known NHLer with his first pro team; in Part 2, match the former NHLer and his last pro team.

(Solutions are on page 116)

Part 1

1. ____	Wayne Gretzky	A.	Toronto Toros
2. ____	Richard Brodeur	B.	Houston Aeros
3. ____	Anders Hedberg	C.	Edmonton Oilers
4. ____	Gordie Roberts	D.	New England Whalers
5. ____	Mike Gartner	E.	Winnipeg Jets
6. ____	Mark Napier	F.	Cincinnati Stingers
7. ____	Michel Goulet	G.	Quebec Nordiques
8. ____	Dave Langevin	H.	Indianapolis Racers
9. ____	Paul Holmgren	I.	Birmingham Bulls
10. ____	Mark Howe	J.	Minnesota Fighting Saints

Part 2

1. ____	Andy Bathgate	A.	Quebec Nordiques
2. ____	Norm Ullman	B.	New York Raiders
3. ____	Frank Mahovlich	C.	New England Whalers
4. ____	Kent Douglas	D.	Los Angeles Sharks
5. ____	J. C. Tremblay	E.	Edmonton Oilers
6. ____	Ted Green	F.	Chicago Cougars
7. ____	Ralph Backstrom	G.	Winnipeg Jets
8. ____	Pat Stapleton	H.	Vancouver Blazers
9. ____	Reggie Fleming	I.	Birmingham Bulls
10. ____	Eric Nesterenko	J.	Cincinnati Stingers

5

OLYMPIC GOLD

What were the final standings in men's hockey at the 1998 Olympics in Nagano, Japan? In this chapter we go for the gold and explore the highs and lows of the first Olympic Games to showcase the NHL's best players. The final medal standings? The gold went to the Czech Republic, the silver to Russia and the bronze to Finland. Highly favoured Team USA and Team Canada both finished out of the medal hunt.

(Answers are on page 57)

5.1 **Which NHL club had the most players named to teams in the 1998 Olympic hockey tournament?**
A. The Detroit Red Wings
B. The New York Rangers
C. The Colorado Avalanche
D. The Philadelphia Flyers

5.2 **NHL players were accused of using what cold medicine as a performance-enhancing drug prior to the 1998 Olympics?**
A. Dristan
B. Advil
C. Sinutab
D. Sudafed

5.3 **Who cross-checked Paul Kariya in the head during an NHL game, forcing him to miss the 1998 Olympics because of a concussion?**
A. Chicago's Gary Suter
B. Washington's Dale Hunter
C. New York's Mike Keane
D. Philadelphia's Joel Otto

5.4 Which Canadian town produced the most members of Team Canada at the 1998 Olympics?

A. St. Foy, Quebec
B. Whitby, Ontario
C. Flin Flon, Manitoba
D. Medicine Hat, Alberta

5.5 What did Wayne Gretzky do to his hockey stick in preparation for the 1998 Olympics?

A. He used white tape instead of his usual black tape
B. He lengthened his stick's shaft
C. He had special markings inscribed on his stick
D. He used a slightly shorter blade to conform to Olympic regulations

5.6 Who scored the most goals at the 1998 Olympics?

A. Wayne Gretzky of Team Canada
B. Philippe Bozon of Team France
C. Pavel Bure of Team Russia
D. Teemu Selanne of Team Finland

5.7 Which NHL player was chosen to represent the Czech Republic at the Nagano Olympics, but couldn't go because of a broken leg?

A. Ottawa's Vaclav Prospal
B. Pittsburgh's Petr Nedved
C. Ottawa's Radek Bonk
D. New Jersey's Bobby Holik

5.8 How many American Hockey League players competed in the 1998 Olympics?

A. None
B. Seven players
C. 14 players
D. 21 players

5.9   Why was Sweden's Ulf Samuelsson disqualified from play
      during the 1998 Olympics?
      A. Because of a horrific on-ice kneeing incident
      B. Because of a citizenship ruling
      C. Because he was caught playing with an illegal stick
      D. Because he tested positive for an illegal drug

5.10 Which player was chosen top defenseman of the Nagano
      Olympics?
      A. Team Canada's Ray Bourque
      B. Team Russia's Darius Kasparaitis
      C. Team Sweden's Nicklas Lidstrom
      D. Team Canada's Rob Blake

5.11 Which sniper blasted a shot so hard it shattered Dominik
      Hasek's helmet during the 1998 Olympics?
      A. Team Canada's Steve Yzerman
      B. Team USA's Brett Hull
      C. Team Russia's Pavel Bure
      D. Team Czech Republic's Jaromir Jagr

5.12 Which Czech player scored in the shootout that eliminated
      Team Canada from gold-medal contention at the 1998
      Olympics?
      A. Robert Reichel
      B. Jaromir Jagr
      C. Martin Straka
      D. Jiri Slegr

5.13 Among the six Canadian NHL teams, which one contributed
      the most Olympians?
      A. The Ottawa Senators
      B. The Montreal Canadiens
      C. The Toronto Maple Leafs
      D. The Edmonton Oilers

5.14 Which team registered the highest percentage of shooting accuracy at the 1998 Olympics?
A. Team Canada
B. Team Russia
C. Team Sweden
D. Team USA

5.15 What NHL team contributed the most players to the American Olympic team?
A. The New York Rangers
B. The Philadelphia Flyers
C. The Chicago Blackhawks
D. The Dallas Stars

5.16 Among all 14 Olympic hockey teams at Nagano, which team handed Dominik Hasek and the Czech Republic their only loss?
A. Team Sweden
B. Team Russia
C. Team USA
D. Team Finland

5.17 Which NHL team contributed the most players to the Olympic gold-medal-winning team from the Czech Republic?
A. The Buffalo Sabres
B. The Pittsburgh Penguins
C. The Dallas Stars
D. The Edmonton Oilers

5.18 Which NHLer scored the goal that clinched the Olympic gold medal for the Czech Republic?
A. Philadelphia's Petr Svoboda
B. Edmonton's Roman Hamrlik
C. The Islanders' Robert Reichel
D. Pittsburgh's Jaromir Jagr

5.19 Which national team placed two players 1-2 in the Olympic scoring race?
A. Team Russia
B. Team Sweden
C. Team Finland
D. Team Canada

5.20 Which national team was featured on a Wheaties cereal box after the 1998 Olympics?
A. The 1998 U.S. Olympic men's hockey team
B. The 1998 Canadian Olympic women's hockey team
C. The 1998 Czech Republic Olympic men's hockey team
D. The 1998 U.S. Olympic women's hockey team

5.21 Which national team created an embarrassing situation by damaging apartments in the Olympic athletes' village?
A. Team Canada
B. Team Russia
C. Team France
D. Team USA

OLYMPIC GOLD
Answers

5.1 C. The Colorado Avalanche
Nine members of the Avalanche played in Nagano in 1998: Canadians Joe Sakic, Patrick Roy and Adam Foote; American Adam Deadmarsh; Russians Valeri Kamensky and Alexei Gusarov; Swede Peter Forsberg; Finn Jari Kuri; and German Uwe Krupp. The Rangers and the Penguins each had eight Olympians; Philadelphia and Chicago, seven.

5.2 D. Sudafed
The Sudafed story surfaced just prior to the 1998 Winter Games when NHL doctors, who oversaw the league's substance-abuse program, met with teams and players to identify banned drugs and testing procedures at the Olympics. Sudafed contains

pseudoephedrine, an IOC-banned substance that stimulates the central nervous system to alleviate colds and congestion. But some NHLers used the over-the-counter drug as a stimulant before games. Since it was considered performance-enhancing by the IOC, any NHLer taking a Sudafed tablet could test positive at the Olympics. No hockey player was banned for drugs and the issue was soon forgotten.

5.3   A. Chicago's Gary Suter
Arguably the best hockey player in the world, Kariya lost his chance to represent Canada at the 1998 Olympics after Suter cross-checked him in the jaw during an Anaheim-Chicago game on February 1, 1998. The dangerous hit, a probable reflex action, came late after Kariya had scored his second goal. "It was a wild scramble and I turned around and I saw a Duck and cross-checked him," Suter said. "He must have crouched down because I didn't hit him that high." Suter, who later received a four-game suspension, also knocked Wayne Gretzky out of the 1991 Canada Cup with a vicious hit from behind. "I was just trying to clear the net. Unfortunately, every time I hit somebody it turns out to be a superstar," said Suter.

5.4   B. Whitby, Ontario
In Team Canada's dressing room at Nagano, the Canadian Hockey Association installed a map of Canada spotted with pins representing each player's hometown. Three players—Keith Primeau, Adam Foote and Joe Nieuwendyk—pinned their names over a small community located just east of Toronto: Whitby, population 65,000. "Having three players from one town the size of Whitby is pretty amazing," Nieuwendyk said.

5.5   C. He had special markings inscribed on his stick
Gretzky took the Olympic symbol and created a new design that incorporated his initials into the five rings. The artwork was marked into the butt of his stick.

5.6 C. Pavel Bure of Team Russia

Bure scored a tournament-high nine goals for Russia, including five goals in a 7-4 win against Finland. Despite his torrid scoring, Bure could not gun one past the Czech Republic's Dominik Hasek in the gold-medal game. Little-knowns Philippe Bozon (France) and Dominic Lavoie (Austria) each scored five goals, but their teams finished out of the medal race. Teemu Selanne (Finland), Konstantin Shafranov (Kazakhstan) and Vlastimil Plavucha (Slovakia) each had four goals.

5.7 A. Ottawa's Vaclav Prospal

Various reasons prevented a number of Czech NHLers from participating at the Olympics. For example, Czech-born Bobby Holik was ineligible because he was a U.S. citizen; Peter Nedved, also ineligible, eliminated himself after winning a silver medal with Canada at the 1994 Games. But Prospal missed his chance for Olympic gold because of a broken fibula, suffered on a hit by Lance Pitlick just a month before the

Games began. Prospal couldn't watch the gold-medal game; he turned it off after five minutes. "I was honoured to be chosen for the team, but it was taken away from me because of the injury," said Prospal.

5.8 B. Seven players

Only seven AHL players appeared in the 1998 Olympics. Syracuse Crunch defenseman Tuomas Gronman of Finland won bronze, the only AHLer to win a medal. In his honour, the Crunch hung the Finnish flag inside Onondaga County War Memorial Arena for the remainder of the 1997-98 season. The other AHL players at the 1998 Olympics: Belarus's Alexei Lojkin (Fredericton), Austria's Martin Hohenberger (Fredericton), Germany's Jan Benda (Portland), Slovakia's Robert Petrovicky (Worcester), Germany's Erich Goldman (Worcester) and Belarus's Alexander Zhurik (Hamilton).

5.9 B. Because of a citizenship ruling

After playing three games at the Olympics, Swedish-born Samuelsson was declared ineligible by the International Ice Hockey Federation because he held both U.S. and Swedish passports. Under Swedish law, dual citizenship is not allowed; once Samuelsson acquired his U.S. passport he automatically lost his Swedish status. The issue was first raised by the Swedish media, who informed the Swedish Ice Hockey Federation. The case went before the IIHF and Samuelsson was barred for the remainder of the Olympics. Team Sweden was allowed to keep its two previous wins, but lost its next game to Finland, eliminating it from medal contention. For the record, a number of Canadians played for Germany and Italy at the Games and were not barred.

5.10 D. Team Canada's Rob Blake

Picked by the tournament directorate as best defenseman, Blake, in six games, took 24 shots on net, scored two points (including a game-winning goal against Sweden), recorded only two penalty minutes and had a tournament-high of +8 in the plus-minus column. Bourque and Kasparaitis also had +8s.

5.11 C. Team Russia's Pavel Bure

During the first Czech Republic-Russia game at the Olympics, Hasek had his helmet shattered by a Pavel Bure slap shot. "I don't care if it's my head that stops the puck," Hasek said. "It's part of my body. If I see the puck coming at my head, I don't move my head. I can make a save with my head also." Hasek wears the old-style wire cage and helmet, instead of the modern NHL wraparound masks sported by netminders such as Patrick Roy and Ed Belfour. After his helmet was smashed, Hasek used an older Buffalo Sabres wire-cage mask.

5.12 A. Robert Reichel

From the opening face-off the Czech Republic-Canada game was a classic goaltender's battle, pitting two net giants, St. Patrick (Patrick Roy) and The Dominator (Dominik Hasek) against each other until the bitter end. After 60 minutes of regulation time and another 10 minutes of overtime, the two clubs were still tied 1-1. To decide the finalist for the gold-medal game, each team selected five players for a shootout. Reichel skated in first and fired a wrist shot to Roy's stick-side. "I was waiting, waiting, and I saw a little spot," said Reichel, whose NHL record on penalty shots is a perfect two for two. Reichel's shot pinged off the post into the net. Each team alternated in penalty-shot format, trying to score another goal. St. Patrick stopped the rest of the Czech shooters, but as good as Roy was, Hasek was better—he blocked all five Canadian shots. Lindros, Canada's third marksman, had the best chance. He faked Hasek cleanly, but his shot hit the post. Brendan Shanahan, who shot fifth, was Canada's last hope. He missed too, outdeked by the Dominator. After the game, Shanahan apologized for "letting the country down. I feel terrible about it." Canada had come to the Olympics to win gold; nothing less. They lost in a shootout. Wayne Gretzky hung his head on the Team Canada bench when it was all over. "This is the worst feeling in the world right now," Gretzky said.

5.13 D. The Edmonton Oilers

Seven Oilers played in Nagano: Bill Guerin and Doug Weight of the United States; Boris Mironov, Andrei Kovalenko and

Valeri Zelepukin of Russia; Mats Lindgren of Sweden; and gold medal-winner Roman Hamrlik of the Czech Republic. Calgary had five players from its club at the Olympics; Toronto, Ottawa and Montreal had four; and Vancouver three.

5.14 B. Team Russia

Based on total shots taken and the total goal count for each team, the Russians fired the most accurate shots at the Olympics. Team Russia connected on 10 per cent of its blasts or 26 times on 261 shots taken. Belarus, which played seven games (they were in the Preliminary Round), had the most shots on net (333); second to Canada's 306. The Americans faired the poorest among all 14 teams, netting only nine goals on 230 shots, or 3.9 per cent.

The Hottest Shots at the 1998 Nagano Olympics

Team	TS	G	Pct.	Team	TS	G	Pct.
1. Russia	261	26	10.0	8. Italy	188	12	6.4
1. Kazakhstan	254	21	8.3	9. Canada	306	19	6.2
2. Finland	267	20	7.5	10. Germany	183	11	6.0
3. Sweden	170	12	7.1	11. Belarus	333	19	5.7
4. Austria	171	12	7.0	12. Japan	162	9	5.6
6. Czech Rep.	271	19	7.0	13. Slovakia	232	11	4.7
7. France	145	10	6.9	14. USA	230	9	3.9

TS/Total shots includes blocked shots, G/Goals, Pct./Team shooting percentage

5.15 C. The Chicago Blackhawks

Three NHL teams provided half the lineup for the Americans. Four Hawks—Tony Amonte, Chris Chelios, Gary Suter and Keith Carney—dressed in the losing cause for Team USA. The Rangers supplied Pat LaFontaine, Brian Leetch and Mike Richter; Dallas contributed Mike Modano, Derian Hatcher and Jamie Langenbrunner. Despite the stellar lineup, the Olympics proved a huge disappointment as the Americans bowed out in a 4-1 quarterfinal loss to the Czech Republic. Modano gave Team USA an early 1-0 lead. But then Dominik Hasek closed the door and turned away 38 of 39 shots. Jaromir Jagr set up ex-NHLer Vladimir Ruzicka to tie the game before he scored the winner himself 58 seconds later. Over the course of the Olympics, the best American scorers were Brett Hull and Bill Guerin, with three points each in four games. Guerin, John LeClair, Keith Tkachuk, Tony Amonte, Doug Weight and Jeremy Roenick all failed to score a goal.

5.16 B. Team Russia
At the 1998 Olympics, Team Czech Republic played six games, winning five and losing only one match, 2-1, to the Russians. Robert Reichel opened the scoring on a second-period power-play goal to give the Czechs a 1-0 lead. But in the third, Russia scored twice in 10 seconds. Valeri Bure tied the game with one of the tournament's prettiest goals. On the rush he split two defensemen, then, while being hooked to the ice, he lifted the puck over a kneeling Hasek. Ten seconds later, Alexei Zhamnov scored the game winner. It was the worst Hasek played during the Olympics. In the next three games, the Dominator allowed only two goals and netted a shutout in the gold-medal game against the Russians. Hasek gave up only six goals in six matches.

5.17 B. The Pittsburgh Penguins
The Czech Republic selected four Penguins to represent its country; as a result, Jaromir Jagr, Martin Straka, Jiri Slegr and Robert Lang all returned to Pittsburgh with gold medals. Only one other NHL team supplied multiple Czech players: Buffalo with Dominik Hasek and Richard Smehlik.

5.18 A. Philadelphia's Petr Svoboda
Svoboda scored the goal of his career when his slap shot from the blueline glanced off a player and flipped over Russian goalie Mikhail Shtalenkov at 8:08 of the third period. It was the only goal the Czechs needed to win their first Olympic gold medal in hockey as Dominik Hasek stoned the Russians with 20 saves in the 1-0 shutout. Svoboda, who defected from the former Czechoslovakia in 1984 to play in the NHL, also holds the

distinction of being the most penalized player at the 1998 Olympics, with 39 minutes. The historic gold-medal goal was his only red light during the tournament.

5.19 C. Team Finland

Finns Teemu Selanne (4-6-10) and Saku Koivu (2-8-10) finished one-two in the Olympic scoring race; each produced 10 points as they led Finland to a bronze-medal finish. Because the Olympic schedule included a preliminary round to determine who would advance to the championship round, the winners, Kazakhstan and Belarus, played seven games while Sweden only had four games before it was eliminated.

The Top 10 Olympic Scorers of 1998

Players	Team	GP	G	A	PTS	PIM
Teemu Selanne	Finland	5	4	6	10	8
Saku Koivu	Finland	6	2	8	10	4
Pavel Bure	Russia	5	9	0	9	2
Alex Koreshkov	Kazakhstan	7	3	6	9	2
Philippe Bozon	France	4	5	2	7	4
Konstan Shafranov	Kazakhstan	7	4	3	7	6
Dominik Lavoie	Austria	4	5	1	6	8
Jere Lehtinen	Finland	6	4	2	6	2
Alexei Yashin	Russia	5	3	3	6	0
Serge Poudrier	France	4	2	4	6	4

5.20 D. The 1998 U.S. Olympic women's hockey team

Wheaties has featured many great athletes on its cereal box since the 1930s, when Johnny Weismuller first endorsed "The Breakfast of Champions." After the Americans beat Canada 3-1 to win the first-ever Olympic gold medal in women's hockey, 15 members of the team posed for the front of the Wheaties box. "Every Olympic athlete's dream. First a gold medal and then your own Wheaties box," said captain Cammi Granato after making one of the most prestigious covers in American sports culture.

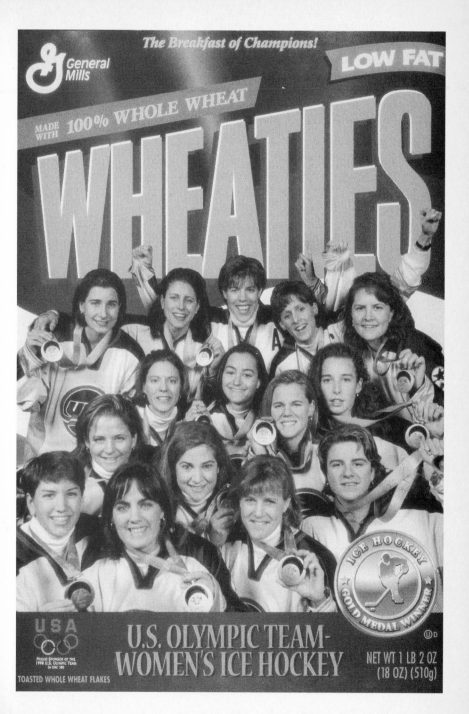

5.21 D. Team USA

In the early hours of February 19, some 12 hours after the Americans were eliminated by the Czech Republic, an unidentified number of U.S. players trashed apartments in the athletes' village by smashing chairs and throwing fire extinguishers out the windows. Estimated damage: $3,000. Captain Chris Chelios, who denied personally causing any of the damage, later apologized for Team USA.

GAME 5

ART ROSS WINNERS

Art Ross brought many things to hockey. More than just a top defenseman during the game's pioneering days, he was a coach, promoter and inventor who improved both the design of the puck and the goal net used in today's NHL. In his honour, the league annually awards its scoring champion the Art Ross Trophy. In this game, find the 18 scoring champs in the puzzle by reading across, down or diagonally. As with our example of Bobby H-U-L-L, connect the last name using letters no more than once. Start with the letters printed in heavy type.

(Solutions are on page 117)

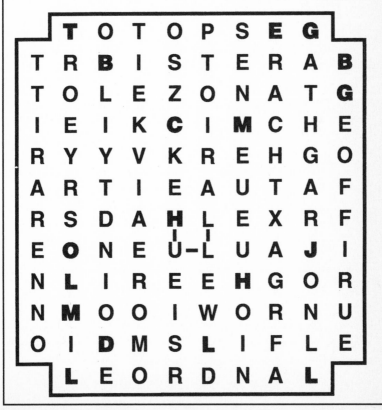

```
T  O  T  O  P  S  E  G
T  R  B  I  S  T  E  R  A  B
T  O  L  E  Z  O  N  A  T  G
I  E  I  K  C  I  M  C  H  E
R  Y  Y  V  K  R  E  H  G  O
A  R  T  I  E  A  U  T  A  F
R  S  D  A  H  L  E  X  R  F
E  O  N  E  U-L  U  A  J  I
N  L  I  R  E  E  H  G  O  R
N  M  O  O  I  W  O  R  N  U
O  I  D  M  S  L  I  F  L  E
   L  E  O  R  D  N  A  L
```

6

TRUE OR FALSE?

Since the advent of the 70-game schedule, only one team, the 1953-54 Chicago Blackhawks, has averaged less than two goals per game in a season. True or False? In this chapter, we ask questions about a variety of hockey subjects, including the Stanley Cup and the 1998 Olympics, all requiring either a true or false response.

As for the question above, it's false. Yes, the 1953-54 Hawks scored just 133 times in 70 matches to average 1.90 goals per game, but in 1997-98, the Tampa Bay Lightning reached new heights of ineptitude by averaging just 1.84 on 151 goals in 82 games, to qualify as the weakest offensive team of modern times.

(Answers are on page 71)

6.1 The Detroit Red Wings have never won a Stanley Cup without a Howe in the team's organization. *True or False?*

6.2 No retired coach has ever won 500 NHL games and *not* been elected to the Hockey Hall of Fame. *True or False?*

6.3 Bobby Orr is the last player to win the NHL scoring title while racking up 100 or more penalty minutes. *True or False?*

6.4 In *The Hockey News'* 1998 poll of the top 50 players of all time, the Montreal Canadiens were the most represented team. *True or False?*

6.5 Mario Lemieux did *not* win the Calder Trophy as rookie of the year. *True or False?*

6.6 Grant Fuhr was the first black player to have his name etched into the Stanley Cup. *True or False?*

6.7 Despite all his scoring records and Stanley Cup championships, Maurice Richard never won the Hart Trophy as league MVP. *True or False?*

6.8 There is no difference in the Olympic rules for men and women's hockey. *True or False?*

6.9 Brett Hull was the only Canadian-born member of Team USA at the 1998 Olympics. *True or False?*

6.10 In Olympic women's hockey, the term defense*man* is used. *True or False?*

6.11 Robert Reichel, the only Czech player to score on Patrick Roy in the shootout that eliminated Team Canada from gold-medal contention at the 1998 Olympics, also scored on his only two NHL penalty shots against Roy. *True or False?*

6.12 Among the four top women's teams at the 1998 Olympics, only one was coached by a man. *True or False?*

6.13 Both the Canadian and American squads at the 1998 Olympics were composed exclusively of NHLers. *True or False?*

6.14 Team USA coach Ron Wilson cut his hair for the elimination game against the Czech Republic at the 1998 Olympics. *True or False?*

6.15 Boston's Ray Bourque is the only defenseman to lead an NHL team in career scoring. *True or False?*

6.16 Wayne Gretzky has more assists than any other NHLer has points. *True or False?*

6.17 Detroit is the only NHL team to retire the sweater numbers of an entire line, in this case, the numbers of Gordie Howe (No.9), Sid Abel (No.12) and Ted Lindsay (No.7). *True or False?*

6.18 The Colorado Avalanche named its mascot "IceMan." *True or False?*

6.19 Dale Hunter is the only NHLer to record 300 goals while never scoring 30 in a season. *True or False?*

6.20 The average height of the Philadelphia Flyers is equal to the height of their football counterparts, the Philadelphia Eagles. *True or False?*

6.21 Mark Messier reached two milestones—his 1,000th assist and his move into fourth place on the NHL all-time scoring list — during the same game in 1997-98. *True or False?*

6.22 Brett Hull was the first player in the 1990s to record three consecutive 50-goal seasons. *True or False?*

6.23 No player who has skated with eight or more NHL teams has ever won the Stanley Cup. *True or False?*

6.24 Kevin Lowe is the only NHLer to play more than 1,000 games for the Edmonton Oilers. *True or False?*

6.25 No defenseman has ever won the Calder Trophy as top rookie and the Norris Trophy as top D-man in the same season. *True or False?*

6.26 Trevor Linden captained the Vancouver Canucks for three seasons before being traded to the New York Islanders in 1997-98. *True or False?*

TRUE OR FALSE?
Answers

6.1 True

As of 1998, the Red Wings had won nine Stanley Cups: three in 1935, 1936 and 1943 with Syd Howe (no relation to Gordie), four in 1950, 1952, 1954 and 1955 with Gordie Howe and in 1997 and 1998 with Mark Howe as a team scout.

6.2 False

Billy Reay earned 542 regular-season wins, a total surpassed by only three NHL coaches: Scotty Bowman, Al Arbour and Dick Irvin. Even so, Reay has not been enshrined in the Hockey Hall of Fame.

6.3 False

Orr, who compiled 101 PIM while winning the Art Ross Trophy in 1974-75, is not the last scoring champ to reach triple digits in box time. Mario Lemieux had exactly 100 PIM when he won the scoring title in 1988-89.

6.4 True

The Canadiens placed 16 players in the hockey publication's top 50 NHLers of all time, including Maurice Richard (No.5), Larry Robinson (No.24) and Patrick Roy (No.34). Boston's seven players ranked next best; then Chicago (five) and Detroit, Edmonton and Toronto (four).

6.5 False

Lemieux won top rookie honours in 1985 with a 43-57-100 record. He was the third rookie to record a 100-point season in NHL history.

6.6 True

Fuhr, the first black player to play for a Stanley Cup winner, claimed four championships with Edmonton, the first Cup coming in 1983-84, when he backstopped the Oilers to 11 playoff victories.

6.7 False

During his stellar 18-year career, Richard set many league records and established a few scoring firsts (50 goals in 50 games). Yet only once did he win MVP honours—in 1947 after scoring 45 goals in the 60-game schedule. The next-best goal scorers that year managed just 30 goals.

6.8 False

There is one major rule difference at the international level. In women's hockey, no intentional body checking is allowed; such contact is penalized with a two-minute minor.

6.9 False

Born in Belleville, Ontario, Hull was one of two Canadian players wearing the red, white and blue instead of the maple leaf at the 1998 Olympics. The other, Adam Deadmarsh of Trail, B.C., shares a similar experience to Hull. Both had dual citizenships and were asked to represent the U.S.—Deadmarsh at the World Juniors in 1993 and Hull at the World Championships in 1986—after not being chosen by Canada for those events. Since international rules stipulate that once a player has played for one country he can not play for another, neither Hull nor Deadmarsh could play for Canada even if they wanted to.

6.10 True

Both terms, defense*man* and lines*man*, are used when women are playing hockey at the Olympic level.

6.11 False

Heading into the Olympics, Reichel had a perfect two-for-two record in penalty-shot goals, but neither one was scored against Roy. Reichel beat Edmonton's Bill Ranford on February 7, 1994, and, later, on October 24, 1996, he scored against Tom Barrasso of Pittsburgh.

6.12 False

There was only one female head coach among the top four women's teams: Shannon Miller of Team Canada. Gold-medal winner Team USA was coached by Ben Smith, Team Finland by Raumo Korpi and Team Sweden by Bengt Ohlson.

6.13 True

All 41 players on Team USA and Team Canada came from the ranks of the NHL.

6.14 True

After seeing his team play poorly in the early rounds, American coach Ron Wilson chopped his hair to a near buzz cut for the elimination game against the Czechs. According to some, Wilson made the change because that was his hairstyle when he coached the Americans to their 1996 World Cup victory. According to Wilson: "My hair is not a concern."

6.15 False

As of 1997-98, Bourque had 375 goals and 1,036 assists for 1,411 points to lead all Bruins in most career points, but he is not the only defenseman to hold his team's career points record. Al MacInnis owns Calgary's mark, with a franchise-high 822 points.

6.16 True

On October 26, 1997, the Great One notched the 1,850th and 1,851st assists of his career to pass Gordie Howe's career mark of 1,850 points. The assist that broke Howe's total was classic Gretzky. He fed Ranger teammate Niklas Sundstrom in the right circle, then circled in behind Sundstrom for a return pass. Gretzky waited briefly, allowing Ulf Samuelsson to join the play late. When Samuelsson skated into the slot, Gretzky pinpointed a perfect pass in front and Samuelsson slammed it past Anaheim's Guy Hebert. A long-standing ovation followed, as Madison Square Garden fans chanted "Gretzky, Gretzky."

6.17 False

The other team to retire an entire line is the Buffalo Sabres, who honoured the French Connection line of Rick Martin (No.7), Gilbert Perreault (No.11) and Rene Robert (No.14).

6.18 False

In 1997, the Avalanche unveiled a new mascot, a seven-foot abominable snowman-like creature called "Howler."

6.19 True

During his 18-plus year, 300-goal career, Hunter's best season count was 28 goals, which he reached twice—with Quebec in 1985-86 and again with Washington in 1991-92.

6.20 False

At six foot three, the average height of the Flyers' team is two inches taller that the Eagles' average of six foot one. However, the Eagles' 241-pound average weight is 33 pounds heavier than the Flyers' average of 208 pounds. Typically, NFLers are on average both taller (six foot two) and heavier (240 pounds) than NHLers.

6.21 False

Messier scored his two milestone points in back-to-back games. He notched his 1,000th assist in a 2-2 tie against Florida on January 10, 1998. On January 12, in his next game, he moved past Phil Esposito into fourth place on the NHL's all-time scoring list with his 1,591th point, an assist in Vancouver's 3-2 loss to Chicago.

6.22 True

Beginning in 1989-90, Hull notched 72-, 86- and 70-goal seasons with St. Louis, to become the first NHLer to manage three straight 50-goal years in the 1990s. Typically, after that hat trick Hull ripped off 54- and 52-goal seasons, giving him a total of five 50-goal seasons in a row.

6.23 False

There are seven players whose careers have taken them to at least eight different NHL teams; two of those have won Stanley Cups on their tour of duty around the league. Larry Hillman won Cups with Detroit (1955), Toronto (1964 and 1967) and Montreal (1969); and Rob Ramage with Calgary (1989) and Montreal (1993).

6.24 True

Lowe holds Edmonton's record for most seasons (15) and most games played (1,037), as of 1997-98. He is the only Oiler with more than 1,000 games to his credit.

6.25 True

Few Calder Trophy winners come from the ranks of defensemen. Only a handful, including Bryan Berard, Denis Potvin and Brian Leetch, have won the award since 1967; none have ever claimed the Calder and Norris during the same season.

6.26 False

Linden was named the Canucks' captain in 1991-92. He wore the "C" for six seasons before voluntarily giving it up to Mark Messier prior to the start of the 1997-98 campaign. The loss of his "C" foreshadowed the end of Linden's nine-and-a-half-year career in Vancouver. In February 1998, the popular forward was traded to the New York Islanders for Todd Bertuzzi and Bryan McCabe.

GAME 6

TEAM IRONMEN

In 25 NHL seasons with Detroit, Gordie Howe played in 1,687 games. It's a team record and a league record for most matches with one team. Now that we've given you that one, match the other 25 NHL teams and the players who hold their clubs' records for most games played.

(Solutions are on page 118)

1.	_____ Anaheim Mighty Ducks	A.	Bobby Clarke
2.	_____ Boston Bruins	B.	Scott Mellanby
3.	_____ Buffalo Sabres	C.	Stan Smyl
4.	_____ Calgary Flames	D.	Neal Broten
5.	_____ Carolina Hurricanes	E.	Gilbert Perreault
6.	_____ Chicago Blackhawks	F.	Henri Richard
7.	_____ Colorado Avalanche	G.	Michel Goulet
8.	_____ Dallas Stars	H.	George Armstrong
9.	_____ Detroit Red Wings	I.	Joe Sacco
10.	_____ Edmonton Oilers	J.	Ron Francis
11.	_____ Florida Panthers	K.	Dave Taylor
12.	_____ Los Angeles Kings	L.	Bryan Trottier
13.	_____ Montreal Canadiens	M.	Gordie Howe
14.	_____ New Jersey Devils	N.	Bernie Federko
15.	_____ New York Islanders	O.	Jean Pronovost
16.	_____ New York Rangers	P.	Thomas Steen
17.	_____ Ottawa Senators	Q.	Rob Zamuner
18.	_____ Philadelphia Flyers	R.	Jeff Odgers
19.	_____ Phoenix Coyotes	S.	Stan Mikita
20.	_____ Pittsburgh Penguins	T.	Alexandre Daigle
21.	_____ St. Louis Blues	U.	Kelly Miller
22.	_____ San Jose Sharks	V.	Al MacInnis
23.	_____ Tampa Bay Lightning	W.	Johnny Bucyk
24.	_____ Toronto Maple Leafs	X.	Harry Howell
25.	_____ Vancouver Canucks	Y.	John MacLean
26.	_____ Washington Capitals	Z.	Kevin Lowe

7

READER REBOUND

In our last hockey trivia book we asked readers to contribute questions by filling out our special form at the back of the book. We received mail from hockey fans all over North America, some of which we've answered in this year's book. Congratulations and thanks to all those who participated—and if you didn't score in this edition, try again next season (see the form at the back of this book).

(Answers are on page 80)

7.1 Which family has had the most brothers play in the NHL? Name them.

Breigh MacKenzie
Cape Breton, Nova Scotia

7.2 Which Ranger scored the series-winning goal against New Jersey that put New York into the Stanley Cup finals in 1994?

Jill DelPozzo
Clifton, New Jersey

7.3 Why are the Montreal Canadiens called the "Habs"?

Stephanie Miskin
Windsor, Ontario

7.4 Which two players were once traded *for* each other in 1991 and then, in 1996, traded *with* each other?

Calvin Bogart
Midland, Texas

7.5 Which St. Louis defenseman tripped up Bobby Orr after Orr had scored the Stanley Cup-winning goal in 1970?

Rhys Richert
Dunnville, Ontario

7.6 Who was San Jose's top draft pick for its inaugural season (1991-92)?

Jon Reynolds
San Leandro, California

7.7 Who won the Calder Trophy as rookie of the year in Wayne Gretzky's first NHL season?

Phil McHugh
Chateauguay, Quebec

7.8 Which goalie led the Ottawa Senators to their first playoff berth in franchise history?

Patrick Melanson
Dieppe, New Brunswick

7.9 Which players assisted Gordie Howe on his last NHL goal?

Bobby Merritt
Livonia, Michigan

7.10 Which player, selected in the first round by the Edmonton Oilers, scored no goals in the season prior to his NHL drafting?

Meg Moquin
Rockaway Beach, New York

7.11 What was Guy Lafleur's nickname?

Derek Voice
Niagara Falls, Ontario

7.12 Which was the first U.S.-based team to win the Stanley Cup?

Hugh Himmel
Lansdale, Pennsylvania
Alex Hartman
Boca Raton, Florida

7.13 What is the most points a player has accumulated in a season without netting a goal?

Norman Autio
Sudbury, Ontario

7.14 Which three players formed the kid line on the 1990 Stanley Cup-winning Edmonton Oilers?

Jason Vansickle
Leduc, Alberta

7.15 Who was the first NHL goalie awarded an assist?

Alisha Ketchabaw
Straffordville, Ontario

7.16 Chicago's Bill Mosienko took 21 seconds to score the NHL's fastest hat trick (in 1952). How many seconds did it take to score the league's *second*-fastest hat trick?

Tyler Paterson
Waterloo, Iowa

7.17 Which NHL team had the most ex-Edmonton Oilers on its roster during one season?

Rory Dlugos
Fairview, Alberta

7.18 Which pair of brothers hold the NHL record for most points in a road game?

Jeremy Gillan
Strathroy, Ontario
Jeff Carpenter
Oromocto, New Brunswick

7.19 Who fired the first regular-season goal in the Florida Panthers' franchise history?

Adam Horner
Kanata, Ontario

7.20 In which season did Wayne Gretzky score his 700th NHL goal?

Stephen Poletto
Cohklih, New York

7.21 What is the most number of minutes played by goalie Felix Potvin in one season?

Beth-Anne Willshire
Drayton, Ontario

7.22 Which current-day NHLer played on every team based in the state of New York during his career?

Rich Jankowski
St. Louis, Missouri

READER REBOUND
Answers

7.1 **The Sutters,** from Viking, Alberta, have produced the most siblings in the NHL. Six brothers—Brian, Darryl, Duane, Brent and twins Rich and Ron—all made it to the big leagues through hustle and tough play.

7.2 **Stephane Matteau** scored sudden-death goals in two multiple-period overtime games against the Devils, including the game seven thriller on May 27, 1994. The goal gave the Rangers a 2-1 win and catapulted them into the Cup finals.

7.3 The Canadiens' nickname, the "Habs," is rooted in a falsehood that dates back to the 1920s, when the team was already wearing the celebrated "CH" crest on its jerseys. American reporters were erroneously told that the "H" stood for the French word for farmers of Quebec, "**habitant**," instead of "Hockey," as in Club de Hockey Canadien. Since the Canadiens had many French players, it was concluded that they came from farms and were, therefore, "habitants," or "Habs."

7.4 Eight players were swapped in the 1991 Pat LaFontaine-Pierre Turgeon trade between the Islanders and the Sabres, including **Randy Wood** to Buffalo and **Benoit Hogue** to New York. Then, in separate deals three months apart in 1995, Toronto traded with the Sabres to get Wood and with the Islanders to

80

get Hogue. Halfway through the next season, in January 1996, the Maple Leafs dealt Wood and Hogue together for Dallas' Dave Gagner. It may be the only time in NHL history that two players, who were once traded for each other, were later traded as teammates.

7.5 Orr's "flying goal," which won Boston the 1970 Stanley Cup, is one of hockey's most enduring images. Photographer Ray Lussier froze the moment, as Orr, with arms outstretched in celebration, was tripped by St. Louis defenseman **Noel Picard** after scoring on Glenn Hall. Orr is literally soaring through the air on the play. Interestingly, there are a number of "fours" associated with Orr's famous goal that both reader Rhys Richert and Ted Wells, a Boston Garden tour guide, have found. Of course, No.4 was Bobby Orr's sweater number, but No.4 was also on Picard's back. The historic goal was Orr's fourth of the playoffs and Boston's fourth of the game, coming in the fourth period (overtime) of a 4-3 score. Boston won the Cup in four straight final games. Orr captured four individual awards that year and the Bruins won 40 games during the season. Also, it was Orr's fourth NHL campaign. Most significantly, the goal was scored at 00:40, giving Boston its first Cup since 1941 and its fourth Cup in franchise history. Had Orr failed on his headlong rush and coughed up the puck in the Blues' zone, according to Orr's defensive partner, Dallas Smith, the result would have been a four-on-one break for St. Louis. But that never happened. Instead, Orr added another chapter to his legend. As Richert pointed out: "All those fours ... it's kind of scary."

7.6 The Sharks' first-ever pick was **Pat Falloon** of the WHL Spokane Chiefs. Falloon was chosen second overall after number one pick Eric Lindros at the 1991 draft.

7.7 Because Gretzky played his first pro year (1978-79) in the WHA, the NHL disqualified him for the Calder Trophy in 1979-80, opening the door to Boston's **Ray Bourque,** who began his Hall of Fame career with a 17-48-65 record and rookie honours.

7.8 **Ron Tugnutt** led Ottawa to its first playoff appearance in 1996-97, by winning seven of the club's last nine regular-season games. He recorded three shutouts during the stretch, won NHL player of the week honours and had a sparkling 1.98 goals-against average after taking over from the injured Damian Rhodes. The Sens' postseason ended in dramatic fashion after a loss in overtime of game seven to the Buffalo Sabres. In the playoffs, Tugnutt recorded one more shutout, his fourth in three weeks. "I don't (usually) get shutouts," Tugnutt said. "This is getting ridiculous."

7.9 Ironically, Gordie Howe scored his last NHL regular-season goal against the Detroit Red Wings, the team for which he played 25 years, won six scoring titles and four Stanley Cups. It was Howe's 801st goal. He scored it on April 6, 1980, on assists by **Ray Allison** and **Gordie Roberts** against Wings goalie Rogie Vachon.

7.10 Despite scoring no goals in 70 games with the OHL Sault St. Marie Greyhounds in 1982-83, the Oilers made **Jeff Beukeboom** their first pick, 19th overall, in the 1983 NHL draft. He may be the only non-goalie ever chosen in the first round who didn't score a goal the season prior to his NHL draft.

7.11 In fact, Guy Lafleur had two official nicknames. In English, Lafleur was always called "**the Flower**," a direct translation of his last name. In his native Quebec, Lafleur's *nom de plume* better captured his most memorable image. The French called him "le Demon Blond" (Blonde Demon), a reference to Lafleur's reckless speed and the blond mane that trailed in his slipstream as he thundered down right wing. Of course, when Guy Lafleur was in full flight, nicknames were forgotten; everyone, French and English, bellowed "Guy! Guy! Guy!"

7.12 Curiously, the last team to win the Stanley Cup before 1917-18, the year the NHL was formed, was the first U.S.-based Cup winner, the Pacific Coast Hockey Association's **Seattle Metropolitans**. Seattle was also the first U.S. team to host a Stanley Cup series. The Metropolitans beat the defending Cup champs, the Montreal Canadiens, 3-1 in the best-of-five finals.

7.13 Reader Norman Autio's answer of Minnesota's Barry Gibbs was incorrect, but it inspired us to find the player who did amass the NHL's greatest goal-less point total in a season. As expected, the culprit is a defenseman: Jim Thomson, a 13-year veteran clutch-and-grabber with Toronto and Chicago from 1945 to 1958. Thomson's stay-at-home style served him well. He captured four Stanley Cups and was named to the Second All-Star Team twice. But he went goal-less for seven seasons, including 1947-48, when he recorded zero goals and **29 assists** in 49 games. Thomson also had two other seasons that rank prominently in the stat box: 0-25-25 in 1951-52 and 0-22-22 in 1952-53; or zero goals and 47 assists in consecutive seasons. During that time he failed to turn on the red light in 139 regular-season games.

Most Points in an NHL Season Without a Goal*					
Player	Year	Team	GP	G	A/PTS
Jim Thomson	1947-48	Toronto	49	0	29
Barry Wilkins	1975-76	Pittsburgh	75	0	27
Jim Thomson	1951-52	Toronto	70	0	25
Craig Ludwig	1982-83	Montreal	80	0	25
Brad McCrimmon	1983-84	Philadelphia	71	0	24
Ott Heller	1938-39	New York	48	0	23
Lee Fogolin	1977-78	Buffalo	76	0	23
Jim Thomson	1952-53	Toronto	69	0	22

Current to 1997-98

7.14 With an average age of 21, the kid line of **Joe Murphy**, **Adam Graves** and **Martin Gelinas** played a crucial role in 1989-90, scoring a combined 30 playoff points as the Oilers won their fifth Stanley Cup championship.

7.15 In old-time hockey, few goalies ever received assists, either because the nature of the game created little opportunity or simply because they were not credited. But there are a few recorded instances of point-scoring goalies. On February 29, 1944, Boston netminder Bert Gardiner connected on a long up-ice pass to Bill Cowley, who raced in on Toronto's Paul Bibeault and scored in the 7-3 loss to the Maple Leafs. Before that, Detroit's Johnny Mowers earned an assist in 1941-42. Even earlier, netminder **Tiny Thompson** of the Boston Bruins was credited with two assists during the 1935-36 season.

7.16 The second-fastest hat trick in league history took just **44 seconds**. Montreal's Jean Béliveau scored at :42, 1:08 and 1:26 of the second period of a game on November 5, 1955, while the Canadiens were holding a two-man advantage against Terry Sawchuk's Detroit Red Wings.

7.17 The **1995-96 St. Louis Blues** may have iced the greatest contingent of ex-Oilers ever assembled. No other NHL team has had more former Oilers on its roster than the Blues had that season. We counted nine: Wayne Gretzky, Shayne Corson, Igor Kravchuk, Mike Hudson, Glenn Anderson, Craig MacTavish, Charlie Huddy, Ken Sutton and Grant Fuhr.

7.18 There are 10 NHLers in the record books with eight-point games, but none of them occurred on the road except the eight-pointers by Quebec's **Peter and Anton Stastny**. In Washington on February 22, 1981, the Nordiques outdueled the Capitals 11-7, as Peter recorded four goals and four assists and brother Anton pumped in three goals and five assists.

7.19 In Florida's first NHL game on October 6, 1993, **Scott Mellanby** scored the Panthers' first franchise goal at 12:31 of the first period in a 4-4 tie with Chicago.

7.20 In **1990-91**, Gretzky captured his ninth scoring title in 11 seasons, scoring his 2,000th career point (October 26, 1990) and 700th career goal (January 3, 1991) en route to a 163-point season. Gretzky's historic marker came against then-Islanders goalie Glenn Healy. He was the fourth NHL player to reach the 700-goal plateau.

7.21 Felix Potvin backstopped Toronto for a league-high 74 games in 1996-97, or **4,271 minutes** between the pipes. During that season, the beleagured Leafs netminder faced an NHL record 2,438 shots.

7.22 **Pat LaFontaine** may be the only NHLer ever to play on all three NHL clubs in New York state. LaFontaine skated with the Islanders, Sabres and Rangers during his career.

GAME 7
MILLENNIUM MEN

Since 1960, when Gordie Howe became the NHL's first 1,000-point player, about 50 NHLers have reached the millennium mark. Listed below are the first names of 27 millennium men. Once you've figured out their family names, find them in the puzzle by reading down, across or diagonally. As with our example of Ray B-O-U-R-Q-U-E, connect the name using letters no more than once. Start with the letters printed in heavy type.

(Solutions are on page 119)

Gordie _____ Jean _____ Alex _____

Norm _____ Stan _____ John _____

Frank _____ Phil _____ Jean _____

Guy _____ Dino _____ Gilbert _____

Darryl _____ Wayne _____ Bryan _____

Bernie _____ Lanny _____ Peter _____

Mark _____ Dale _____ Mike _____

Ray _____ Mario _____ Glenn _____

Steve _____ Bobby _____ Brian _____

B	K	I	M	P	A	S	T	N	Y	T	R	A	G
E	I	R	E	T	R	Q	U	R	E	N	Y	E	L
T	L	R	S	U	L	C	I	E	C	K	R	I	L
A	F	I	E	O	E	I	E	C	Z	A	P	O	R
D	E	A	V	B	M	X	U	T	D	E	R	P	P
R	E	K	U	E	G	R	E	N	H	O	W	S	N
E	K	E	R	L	A	D	A	E	R	K	E	R	O
O	L	N	A	T	R	U	L	I	S	S	U	H	E
Y	K	L	A	L	C	E	A	N	O	E	H	C	I
C	U	E	M	R	E	Z	L	O	M	T	A	R	T
D	B	T	E	U	R	Y	T	C	D	I	W	E	T
E	A	L	C	H	I	O	M	T	M	S	T	R	O
L	R	C	F	A	M	U	A	I	S	O	P	S	H
V	E	L	A	N	L	L	H	O	V	L	I	C	E

8

BEYOND THE BOARDS

Not all the action in hockey takes place on the ice. Sometimes the best plays happen away from the rink. For example, four prominent free agents—Sergei Fedorov, Paul Kariya, Petr Nedved and Oleg Tverdovsky—all went unsigned long into 1997-98. The situation affected both their teams' on-ice performances and important off-ice matters, such as league salary scales.

In this chapter we test your hockey acumen on a variety of hockey-related subjects beyond the bounds of the boards. So, which free agent held out longest? Among our four, only Nedved's price remained too high, driving away other clubs and potential offers after he turned down a three-year, $15-million deal from Pittsburgh. While Kariya, Fedorov and Tverdovsky skated, Nedved sat out and missed 1997-98.

(Answers are on page 92)

8.1 *The Hockey News'* 1998 poll of the top 50 players of all time ranked Wayne Gretzky the NHL's number one player. Who finished second?
A. Maurice Richard
B. Bobby Orr
C. Mario Lemieux
D. Gordie Howe

8.2 To what charitable cause did Ottawa Senator Alexei Yashin donate $1 million in 1998?
A. To the arts: Ottawa's National Arts Centre
B. To hockey: Russia's Ice Hockey Federation
C. To medical research: Canada's Neurological Institute for Research into Head Injuries
D. To missing children: The Missing Children's Network

8.3 At the 1998 NHL All-Star game a lucky fan had the opportunity to win $5 million if he hit four targets hanging in the corners of a hockey net. How many targets did he hit?
   A. One target
   B. Two targets
   C. Three targets
   D. He missed every target

8.4 How long was Paul Kariya's much-publicized contract holdout during the 1997-98 season?
   A. Two games
   B. 12 games
   C. 32 games
   D. 52 games

8.5 How long was Alan Eagleson sentenced to prison after he pleaded guilty to hockey-related fraud charges in 1997?
   A. 18 days
   B. 18 weeks
   C. 18 months
   D. 18 years

8.6 Which NHL Hall of Famer first vowed publicly to quit the Hockey Hall of Fame if Alan Eagleson was allowed to remain a member?
   A. Brad Park
   B. Carl Brewer
   C. Bobby Orr
   D. Gordie Howe

8.7 What job was Alan Eagleson assigned when he was imprisoned in 1998?
   A. Cook
   B. Cleaner
   C. Librarian
   D. Coach of the prison hockey team

8.8 Which NHL coach wrote a weekly column for *The Sporting News* in 1997-98?
A. Boston's Pat Burns
B. Dallas' Ken Hitchcock
C. Vancouver's Mike Keenan
D. Detroit's Scotty Bowman

8.9 On January 9, 1998, a naked fan streaked across the ice at Calgary's Saddledome during overtime of a Flames-Panthers game. Which song did the public-address system play to accompany the streaker?
A. The Village People's "Macho Man"
B. David Rose's "The Stripper"
C. Carly Simon's "You're So Vain"
D. Tina Turner's "Simply the Best"

8.10 What important hockey site is located at 42 Varadi Avenue?
A. Don Cherry's first bar/restaurant
B. The Hockey Hall of Fame
C. The NHL Player's Association
D. Wayne Gretzky's childhood home

8.11 What does Teemu Selanne collect?
A. Automobiles
B. Hockey cards
C. Toy soldiers
D. Movie star autographs and memorabilia

8.12 How did retired great Bryan Trottier respond when asked if he missed playing hockey?
A. "It's time to pass the torch."
B. "Only when my knees don't hurt."
C. "Six Cups is plenty for one fella."
D. "Only every day."

8.13 Which beer maker produced a 1998 television commercial in which a spontaneous road-hockey game breaks out on a busy city street?
A. Molson
B. Budweiser
C. Labatt
D. Coors

8.14 Who was the first player to admit publicly to participating in the NHL's substance-abuse program?
A. Brett Thomas
B. Ken Daneyko
C. Randy Ellis
D. Réne Lacroix

8.15 What was the lowest salary earned by a hockey player signed to an NHL contract in 1997-98?
A. $100,000 to $150,000
B. $150,000 to $200,000
C. $200,000 to $250,000
D. $250,000 to $300,000

8.16 Which hockey player was voted Canada's top newsmaker of 1997?
A. Mario Lemieux
B. Wayne Gretzky
C. Eric Lindros
D. Sheldon Kennedy

8.17 Which big-name country and western singer helped promote the Nashville Predators in a 1997-98 advertising campaign?
A. Garth Brooks
B. Tricia Yearwood
C. Shania Twain
D. Clint Black

8.18 As of 1997-98, which NHL team's home arena was involved in the richest stadium naming-rights contract?
A. The Vancouver Canucks'
B. The Chicago Blackhawks'
C. The Los Angeles Kings'
D. The Washington Capitals'

8.19 In which season did Vincent Damphousse miss his first game due to injury?
A. His first NHL season (1986-87)
B. His fourth NHL season (1989-90)
C. His eighth NHL season (1993-94)
D. His 12th NHL season (1997-98)

8.20 Nashville's NHL expansion team, the Predators, has what kind of animal on its logo?
A. A screaming eagle
B. A sabre-toothed tiger
C. A grizzly bear
D. A Tyrannosaurus Rex

8.21 Among the six NHL coaches fired in 1997-98, how many were from the league's Atlantic Division?
A. Two coaches
B. Three coaches
C. Four coaches
D. Five coaches

BEYOND THE BOARDS
Answers

8.1 **B. Bobby Orr**
To celebrate its 50th anniversary in 1998, *The Hockey News* polled 50 hockey experts to determine the NHL's top 50 players of all time. Gretzky finished first with 2,726 voter points, followed closely by Bobby Orr (2,713 points). While Orr finished just 13 points behind Gretzky, Gordie Howe was only 32 points

behind Orr with 2,681. Mario Lemieux was fourth with 2,308 points and Maurice Richard fifth with 2,142 points.

8.2   A. To the arts: Ottawa's National Arts Centre

Hockey players have often made charitable contributions to medical research and children's organizations, but Yashin's donation of $1 million to the National Arts Centre in 1998 is the first of its kind in the NHL. Rarely do the arts receive such contributions from players. "We do make a lot of money and I think it's great when we can give back to the community," said Yashin, Ottawa's highest-paid player at $18 million over four years. "I'm glad to give to Ottawa because Ottawa gives a lot to me, too." There were no conditions attached to the donation, though Yashin did swap his stick for a baton to help conduct the NAC's rendition of CBC's *Hockey Night in Canada* theme song before an audience of hockey fans on a school trip in March 1998.

8.3   D. He missed every target

Wayne King, a 37-year-old electronics technician from Dayton, Ohio, had the chance of a lifetime to win a million dollars a target and a bonus of $1 million if he hit all four targets at the 1998 NHL All-Star game. Standing on a rubber mat 31 feet from the net, King had eight seconds to hit the targets. But he blew it, never once raising the puck off the ice. He took home $10,000 dollars for participating in the event, sponsored by Norelco razors.

8.4   C. 32 games

Kariya lost almost half of the 1997-98 season due to his contract dispute with the Disney-owned Mighty Ducks. Anaheim wanted its star centre to sign a multiyear offer, but Kariya was looking for a short-term deal, one that wouldn't restrict future earnings. Disney's hard line held until December 1997, when Kariya was scheduled to join Canada's national team in Europe as part of a training effort to get him ready for the Nagano Olympics. Had he not signed then, the result may have been an Anaheim franchise without Kariya for the season—or forever. But Kariya's power play paid off. He inked a two-year pact worth $5.5 million in 1997-98 and $8.5 million in the next season. After the signing someone in the Ducks organization joked: "He better just show up for practice tomorrow." Kariya did and played 22 games before a Gary Suter cross-check sidelined him for the remainder of the regular season. Kariya played just 22 games in 1997-98. The Ducks were 11-15-6 without Kariya during his contract dispute; a disappointing 6-13-3 with him in the next 22 games; and, after his injury, 9-15-4 to close out the season.

8.5   C. 18 months
Alan Eagleson, once hockey's most powerful man, built the game as an agent, founder of the players' union and chief organizer of international hockey. But dogged investigative work by *Lawrence Eagle-Tribune* writer Russ Conway led to Eagleson's 1997 criminal prosecution on fraud and theft charges. After pleading guilty in Boston and Toronto courts, Eagleson was fined $1 million and sentenced to 18 months in jail for swindling players, stealing disability-insurance money and theft of profits from various Canada Cup hockey tournaments (money intended for the players' pension fund).

8.6   A. Brad Park
Before Eagleson resigned from the Hockey Hall of Fame on March 25, 1998, a total of 18 Hall of Famers stepped forward and threatened to quit the Hall if the board of directors let Eagleson stay. Among those seeking Eagleson's disbarment was Brad Park, a premier defenseman during the 1970s and 1980s and the first to challenge the Hall publicly to oust Eagleson. Just weeks before the Hall was to decide his fate, Eagleson resigned rather than let the Hall "suffer as a result of more controversy." The resignation was the first in the Hall's history and is thought to be the first by any member of any major sports hall of fame.

8.7   B. Cleaner
Eagleson was assigned to fetch coffee and work as a cleaner in a Toronto-area prison office where staff oversee electronic

monitoring of inmates and the temporary-absence program. Jobs with low physical demands are usually reserved for older inmates like Eagleson, who was 64 at the time.

8.8 C. Vancouver's Mike Keenan

Keenan began doing his "Inside the Game" column for the sports weekly at the start of the 1997-98 NHL season, when he was unemployed, and he continued to do so after he was hired as head coach of Vancouver in November 1997. Iron Mike didn't actually write the column himself; he had a writer at the paper translate his comments into print. Keenan discussed a variety of topics in his column, including methods of motivating players, the role of team leaders and the reason why he publicly criticized Trevor Linden.

8.9 A. The Village People's "Macho Man"

With 1:22 remaining in overtime, spectator Julian Vaudrey, 21, jumped the glass and ran around the rink wearing only a smile and a whistle for almost four minutes. He then stopped at centre ice to wave to 17,000 roaring fans. Calgary's public-address officials got into the act, playing the disco hit "Macho Man" before security escorted Vaudrey to a dressing room. Florida Panther Kirk Muller laughed 'til he cried and said, "I knew the guy had to be from up here [Calgary] because he didn't have a very good tan."

8.10 D. Wayne Gretzky's childhood home

The house at 42 Varadi Avenue in Brantford, Ontario, earned a place in hockey lore because of the rink that Walter Gretzky installed in his backyard. It was where No.99 learned to skate. The neighbourhood kids used to call it "Wally Coliseum."

8.11 A. Automobiles

At last count, Selanne had 23 cars and trucks in his impressive automobile collection, including the truck he won after being named MVP at the 1998 NHL All-Star game.

8.12 D. "Only every day."

Trottier squeezed every last game out of his tired legs before he quit his 18-year NHL career in 1993-94. Even then he was just hanging on, a shadow of his former self during his glory years as scoring ace and inspirational leader of the 1980s Islanders' four-in-a-row championship teams. "He had nice soft hands but he could also knock over a moose," former Islanders general manager Bill Torrey once said. When Trottier's numbers began to dwindle, the power forward signed as a free agent with Pittsburgh in 1990, a move that helped the Pens win two consecutive Stanley Cups. Although he scored only seven points in each postseason, his big heart and experience as a Cup champion well ever present on the Mario Lemieux-led Penguins. Unlike Lemieux, who retired early, Trottier would rather be playing (than coaching the American League's Portland Pirates). He was NHL rookie of the year in 1976, once led the NHL in scoring, twice led in assists, twice led the playoffs in scoring, was league MVP in 1978-79 and playoff MVP the next year. He scored 524 goals and 1,425 points in 1,279 games. Trottier was elected to the Hockey Hall of Fame in 1997, his first year of eligibility.

8.13 C. Labatt

The ad, part of Labatt's "Out of the Blue" marketing campaign, starts with a young man flicking a crumpled can at the feet of a passerby on a busy street. Both men have hockey sticks and a road-hockey game ensues. Another businessman gets into it by playing goalie, using his umbrella and briefcase as a stick and blocker and a bicycle rack as his net. Other pedestrians join in to play or cheer before someone yells "Streetcar!"—ending the game. The spot was shot in mid-January in Toronto. The soundtrack is the hockey-arena anthem "Rock and Roll, Part II," by Gary Glitter.

8.14 B. Ken Daneyko

Devils mainstay Ken Daneyko voluntarily turned himself over to the NHL's substance-abuse program in November 1997, becoming the first "known" NHLer to take part in the no-fault rehab plan run jointly by the league and the players' association. "I'm an alcoholic, I cannot drink," he said in 1998. "It took me a long time to admit that to myself, much less anyone else. I'd been getting by, faking it, but hockey was the only good thing I was doing." According to Daneyko, he never drank heavily before a game or played drunk. "The only control in my life was hockey." As of 1997-98, Daneyko leads the Devils in most seasons (15) played, skating in every New Jersey season except the franchise's first, 1982-83. (The other three multiple-choice players in our question are fictitious.)

8.15 C. $200,000 to $250,000

In 1997-98, Czech-born Ladislav Benysek of the AHL's Hamilton Bulldogs, the Edmonton Oilers' farm team, earned $235,000 and the dubious distinction of making less money than all the other 633 pros signed to NHL contracts. Upon hearing that he topped the annual salary of Canada's Prime Minister Jean Chretien, the rookie defenseman advised Chretien in halting English: "Learn to skate. Get raise that way." The issue gained attention when Chretien, trying to justify a wage hike for MPs, complained that his $163,620 salary pay cheque had him "making less that the worst player in the NHL."

8.16 D. Sheldon Kennedy

Newspaper editors and broadcast news directors voted Kennedy Canada's top newsmaker of 1997, citing his courage in going public about the years of sexual abuse he endured from junior coach Graham James. In a year of hockey-related sex-abuse scandals, Sheldon Kennedy gave the sport back its dignity, the editors remarked. As a result, Kennedy's bravery inspired other men to come forward with their own stories of abuse. Kennedy played with Detroit, Calgary and Boston, before retiring in 1997 to run a treatment facility for sexually abused youngsters in British Columbia.

8.17 A. Garth Brooks

To promote their premier NHL season, the Nashville Predators recruited Brooks and other celebrities, such as Amy Grant and

Vince Gill, to pose for print ads that showed each of them with their front teeth blacked out. The ad slogan read "Got Tickets?"—a take-off on the familiar "Got Milk?" campaign that features famous people with milk mustaches.

8.18 C. The Los Angeles Kings'
Although more that 40 North American arenas and stadiums have naming-rights contracts, none compare to the 20-year, $100-million deal signed in December 1997 between the L.A. Arena Co. and Staples, the office-supply retail chain, to put their name and logo on the future home of the Kings and NBA's Lakers. It was the highest paying such agreement to date, but far from covered construction costs. The L.A. Arena Co. borrowed $305 million from the Bank of America, another first considering the loan is the largest private funding deal for a U.S. sports arena.

8.19 D. His 12th NHL season (1997-98)
For the first time since joining the league in 1986, Damphousse missed a game due to injury on March 11, 1998, his 12th season. In his entire career he sat out only eight games: five with Toronto as a healthy scratch in 1987-88, and three more due to suspensions—one in 1990-91 with the Leafs and two in 1995-96 with Montreal. Damphousse missed the March 11 game after hurting his shoulder two nights earlier in a 6-1 Montreal victory against the Florida Panthers.

8.20 B. A sabre-toothed tiger
Market research and fan balloting helped name the Nashville NHL franchise, the Predators. The club's logo is a dramatic profile of a sabre-toothed tiger, which in prehistoric times was native to the area that is now Nashville.

8.21 D. Five coaches
During 1997-98, an epidemic of bench firings swept through the weak Atlantic Division, knocking out five coaches in the seven-team NHL division. Florida replaced Doug MacLean with Bryan Murray; Tampa Bay's Terry Crisp vacated the

bench for Jacques Demers; Wayne Cashman was demoted by the Flyers to bring in Roger Neilson; the New York Rangers let go Colin Campbell for John Muckler; and the Islanders' Rick Bowness was replaced by Mike Milbury. The five firings in the Atlantic Division might be a record, if any statistics in this category were kept. Only one other coach was canned during the 1997-98 regular season. In the Pacific Division, the Vancouver Canucks hired Mike Keenan to replace Tom Renney.

GAME 8
THE ALL-TIME TOP TWENTY

In 1997-98 *The Hockey News* conducted a poll among hockey experts to determine the top 50 players of all time. In our game below match the 20 top-ranked players in the left column and their first NHL season of 25 games or more. Three players began their careers in 1979-80.

(Solutions are on page 120)

1. _____	Wayne Gretzky	A.	1923-24
2. _____	Bobby Orr	B.	1926-27
3. _____	Gordie Howe	C.	1943-44
4. _____	Mario Lemieux	D.	1946-47
5. _____	Maurice Richard	E.	1947-48
6. _____	Doug Harvey	F.	1950-51
7. _____	Jean Béliveau	G.	1953-54
8. _____	Bobby Hull	H.	1954-55
9. _____	Terry Sawchuk	I.	1955-56
10. _____	Eddie Shore	J.	1957-58
11. _____	Guy Lafleur	K.	1959-60
12. _____	Mark Messier	L.	1963-64
13. _____	Jacques Plante	M.	1966-67
14. _____	Ray Bourque	N.	1971-72
15. _____	Howie Morenz	O.	1973-74
16. _____	Glenn Hall	P.	1977-78
17. _____	Stan Mikita	Q.	1979-80
18. _____	Phil Esposito	R.	1979-80
19. _____	Denis Potvin	S.	1979-80
20. _____	Mike Bossy	T.	1984-85

9

SILVER CHASE

During the 1992 Stanley Cup playoffs, the Chicago Blackhawks became the first team in NHL history to win 11 consecutive playoff games. A few days later, the Pittsburgh Penguins duplicated the feat of 11 straight postseason victories, ironically enough, by sweeping the Blackhawks in four straight games in the Cup finals.

In this final chapter, we check out some more playoff firsts and a few amazing team records from the 30-year span from 1967-68 to 1996-97.

(Answers are on page 106)

9.1   As of 1997-98, how many playoff points does Wayne Gretzky have in 16 years of postseason action?
A. Between 250 and 300 points
B. Between 300 and 350 points
C. Between 350 and 400 points
D. More than 400 points

9.2   In the balloting for the 1997 Conn Smythe Trophy (playoff MVP) how many more votes did Detroit goalie Mike Vernon receive than captain Steve Yzerman? (There were 14 ballots cast.)
A. Two votes more
B. Four votes more
C. Six votes more
D. Eight votes more

9.3   What is the NHL record for the fastest two goals by one player in the playoffs?
A. Five seconds
B. 15 seconds
C. 25 seconds
D. 35 seconds

9.4 Which was the last team composed entirely of Canadian-born players to win the Stanley Cup?
A. The 1975 Philadelphia Flyers
B. The 1977 Montreal Canadiens
C. The 1980 New York Islanders
D. The 1989 Calgary Flames

9.5 In the six years between 1992 and 1997, there were six different Stanley Cup champions. When, if ever, has there been a streak like this before in league action?
A. In the 1930s
B. In the 1950s
C. In the 1970s
D. It has never happened before

9.6 How old was the oldest NHLer to play on a Stanley Cup champion?
A. 37 years old
B. 42 years old
C. 47 years old
D. 52 years old

9.7 Who was the first American-born player to score a hat trick in a Stanley Cup final-series game?
A. The Islanders' Ken Morrow
B. Philadelphia's Paul Holmgren
C. Minnesota's Neal Broten
D. Pittsburgh's Joe Mullen

9.8 In 30 years of NHL postseason action between 1968 and 1997, how many teams made the playoffs each and every season during that span?
A. None
B. Only one team, the Boston Bruins
C. Three teams
D. Five teams

9.9   In 30 years of NHL postseason action between 1968 and 1997,
      which team won the most playoff games?
      A. The Boston Bruins
      B. The Philadelphia Flyers
      C. The Edmonton Oilers
      D. The Montreal Canadiens

9.10 In 30 years of NHL postseason action between 1968 and 1997,
      which team played the most games during one playoff season,
      without making the Cup finals in that year?
      A. The 1990 Chicago Blackhawks
      B. The 1993 Toronto Maple Leafs
      C. The 1994 New Jersey Devils
      D. The 1996 Detroit Red Wings

9.11 In 30 years of NHL postseason action between 1968 and 1997,
      which finalist played the most playoff games only to lose the
      Stanley Cup?
      A. The 1986 Calgary Flames
      B. The 1987 Philadelphia Flyers
      C. The 1991 Minnesota North Stars
      D. The 1994 Vancouver Canucks

9.12 In 30 years of NHL postseason action between 1968 and 1997,
      what is the best record (fewest losses) by a Stanley Cup
      champion under the playoff format of four rounds of seven
      games each?
      A. 16 wins, no losses
      B. 16 wins, two losses
      C. 16 wins, four losses
      D. 16 wins, six losses

9.13 Which was the first former WHA club to win the Stanley
      Cup?
      A. The Winnipeg Jets
      B. The Hartford Whalers
      C. The Quebec Nordiques
      D. The Edmonton Oilers

9.14 Who was the first former WHA player to score a Stanley Cup-winning goal after the NHL and WHA merged in 1979-80?
A. Ken Linseman
B. Mark Messier
C. Dave Hunter
D. Wayne Gretzky

9.15 Who is the only rookie to record double-digit goal totals in his first playoffs after playing fewer than 20 regular-season games?
A. Chicago's Jeremy Roenick
B. The Islanders' Pat Flatley
C. Montreal's Claude Lemieux
D. Minnesota's Dino Ciccarelli

9.16 As of the 1998 playoffs, how many Stanley Cups had coach Scotty Bowman won, and with how many different teams?
A. Six Cups with two different teams
B. Seven Cups with three different teams
C. Eight Cups with three different teams
D. Nine Cups with four different teams

9.17 How many modern-day players (since 1943-44 when the redline was introduced) have won the Stanley Cup with at least three different teams?
A. Two players
B. Five players
C. 10 players
D. 20 players

9.18 How many family members of Detroit Red Wings owner Mike Ilitch got their names inscribed on the Stanley Cup when Detroit won the silverware in 1997?
A. Two family members
B. Four family members
C. Six family members
D. Eight family members

9.19 Who is the only player in NHL history to win both league MVP awards—the Hart Trophy (regular season) and the Conn Smythe (playoffs)—in the same season, and then repeat the feat a second time?
A. Bobby Orr
B. Guy Lafleur
C. Wayne Gretzky
D. Mario Lemieux

9.20 Which NHL coach publicly complained during the 1998 playoffs about the FOX puck?
A. Washington's Ron Wilson
B. Buffalo's Lindy Ruff
C. Detroit's Scotty Bowman
D. Dallas' Ken Hitchcock

9.21 As of 1998, how many team captains have won the Conn Smythe Trophy as the most valuable player of the playoffs since the award was first presented in 1965?
A. Three captains
B. Five captains
C. Seven captains
D. Nine captains

9.22 Which dynasty teams produced the most NHL team and individual offensive playoff records?
A. Toronto's dynasty teams of the 1940s
B. Montreal's dynasty teams of the 1970s
C. The Islanders' dynasty teams of the 1980s
D. Edmonton's dynasty teams of the 1980s

SILVER CHASE
Answers

9.1 C. Between 350 and 400 points
The Great One not only owns many of the NHL's regular-season scoring records but many playoff marks as well, including most goals (122), most assists (260) and most points (382) in the postseason. Gretzky's dominance is unlikely to be challenged soon. His next closest rival, Mark Messier, has 295 points; a staggering 87 playoff points behind Gretzky. Besides Messier, three other colleagues from Gretzky's Oiler days round out the top five: Jari Kurri (233 points), Glenn Anderson (214) and Paul Coffey (195). Incredibly, Gretzky has racked up more playoff points than Jean Béliveau and Gordie Howe combined.

9.2 A. Two votes more
The 1997 balloting for playoff MVP proved to be the closest vote in the award's history. Fourteen members of the Professional Hockey Writers' Association cast their ballots and after the smoke cleared Vernon had received two more votes than Yzerman. Vernon finished the postseason with a 16-4 won-lost record and a 1.76 goals-against average (he allowed two goals or fewer in 17 of his 20 playoff games). Although a $10,000 prize accompanied the award, Vernon also earned a cool $200,000 contract bonus.

9.3 A. Five seconds
Detroit Red Wings centre Norm Ullman unleashed the two fastest playoff goals in NHL annals on April 11, 1965, against goalie Glenn Hall of Chicago. Ullman scored at 17:35 and 17:40 of the second period in the fifth game of the semifinals. Detroit won the match 4-2, but lost the playoff round to the Blackhawks.

9.4 A. The 1975 Philadelphia Flyers
The infamous Broad Street Bullies club was the last all-Canadian-born contingent of players to win the Stanley Cup. All of the other teams in the question had non-Canadians in

their lineups. The 1977 Montreal Canadiens iced American-born Bill Nyrop and Mike Polich and Venezuelan-born Rick Chartraw; the 1980 Islanders sported Stefan Persson, Bob Nystrom and Anders Kallur of Sweden; and the 1989 Flames had Americans Joe Mullen and Gary Suter and Swede Hakan Loob.

9.5   A. In the 1930s
When Pittsburgh, Montreal, New York, New Jersey, Colorado and Detroit each won a Stanley Cup between 1992 and 1997, they tied the longest Cup streak in league history: six different champions in six years. The only other such streak dates back to the 1930s, when the Montreal Canadiens (1931), Toronto Maple Leafs (1932), New York Rangers (1933), Chicago Blackhawks (1934), Montreal Maroons (1935) and Detroit Red Wings (1936) each captured the championship. Coincidentally, the Detroit Red Wings ended both streaks, winning back-to-back championships in 1936 and 1937, and then again, 61 years later, in 1997 and 1998.

9.6   B. 42 years old
When Russia's Viacheslav Fetisov won the Stanley Cup with the Detroit Red Wings in 1998, he was 40 years and two months old. But Fetisov still ranks third among the most senior Cup winners. The second-oldest player was defenseman Allan Stanley, who, at 41 years and two months, was a winner with Toronto in 1967. But no player tops Stanley's teammate, Leaf goalie Johnny Bower, who at 42 years and six months, also sipped champagne in 1967. The 1967 Leaf squad sported the oldest lineup ever to win a Stanley Cup. The team had seven players over 35 and 12 members over 30.

9.7   B. Philadelphia's Paul Holmgren
Minnesota-born Paul Holmgren became the first American to score three goals in a final-series game during the 1980 Stanley Cup playoffs. A blue-blood Flyer, Holmgren's gritty play proved an invaluable asset, as he posted 10 goals and added 10 assists during the postseason. His hat trick came in game two

of the finals against the Islanders' Billy Smith, who was chased from the net as Holmgren popped a goal in each period of the Flyers' 8-3 win.

9.8   A. None
Because expansion in 1967-68 increased league size to 12 teams, only those dozen teams qualify for this answer. But none succeeded in making the playoffs every season during the 30-year period. The Boston Bruins, who hold the league record for most consecutive playoff appearances (29), missed only one postseason, the last and 30th year, 1996-97. The Chicago Blackhawks also fell short by only one season after failing to qualify for postseason action in 1968-69. The Canadiens missed two seasons, the Blues three and the Rangers four.

9.9   D. The Montreal Canadiens
Since Boston recorded the most consecutive playoff years (29) during the 30-year span, the Bruins would be a good guess with 152 wins. But they can't match the success of the Canadiens, who earned 211 wins and 10 Stanley Cups in that time. The Philadelphia Flyers rank the highest of all expansion teams on the playoff victory chart, with 144 wins.

The NHL's Top Playoff Team Records
1967-68 to 1996-97

Team	MPS*	Wins	Losses	Cups
Montreal	2	211	120	10
Boston	1	152	144	2
Philadelphia	6	144	129	2
Islanders	8	128	90	4
Edmonton	5	127	67	5
Chicago	1	125	141	0
Rangers	4	116	130	1
St. Louis	3	105	130	0

*MPS/Number of missed playoff seasons

9.10 B. The 1993 Toronto Maple Leafs

In the era of best-of-seven series for four rounds, any team that qualifies for the third round (Conference finals) but not the Stanley Cup finals, can play a potential maximum of 21 games—by stretching each of the three series to the seventh and deciding game. Only one team, the 1993 Maple Leafs, maxed the 21-game limit without making the Cup finals. In the Division semis, Toronto squeaked by Detroit, winning game seven in overtime; then, in the Division finals, the Leafs prevailed over St. Louis in seven games; and in the Conference finals, Toronto lost a seventh-game heartbreaker 5-4 to Wayne Gretzky's Kings.

9.11 B. The 1987 Philadelphia Flyers

Based on seven games in each of four playoff rounds, the maximum number of matches for any Cup finalist is 28 games. No team has ever been pushed to a seventh and deciding game in every playoff round, but the 1987 Flyers played two six-game series and two seven-game series for a total of 26 games without claiming the Stanley Cup. Other marathon teams that went Cup-less include: the 1994 Canucks at 24 games; the 1993 Kings (24 games); the 1991 North Stars (23 games); and the 1986 Flames (22 games).

9.12 B. 16 wins, two losses

No Stanley Cup winner in any postseason format since 1967 has ever swept the championship. Montreal lost only one game in its 1968 and 1976 championships, but those series were contested under less rigorous playoff formats. Since the NHL began the four rounds of best-of-seven series concept in 1987, no team can match Edmonton's 16-2 count of 1988. The Oilers lost once to Winnipeg in the Division semis; took four straight from Calgary in the Division finals; lost another game to Detroit in the Conference finals; and won the Cup in four straight final matches over Boston. Edmonton's 18-game romp to the Stanley Cup in 1988 is the fastest of all Cup champs to date.

9.13 D. The Edmonton Oilers

The Oilers, who joined the NHL in 1979-80, along with the Nordiques, Whalers and Jets, became the first WHA team to win the Stanley Cup in 1983-84, their fifth NHL season. Six players—Wayne Gretzky, Mark Messier, Dave Hunter, Willy Lindstrom, Ken Linseman and Dave Semenko—or 30 per cent of the roster, were WHA alumni, including coach Glen Sather, who played in one WHA Oiler season, 1976-77, and assistant coach Ted Green, a seven-year WHA veteran.

9.14 A. Ken Linseman

Three former WHA players have scored Stanley Cup winners: Messier (1994), Gretzky (1988) and Linseman, who bagged the first Oiler Cup-winning goal on May 19, 1984. Linseman was drafted by Birmingham as an underage junior, and recorded a 38-38-76 rookie season in 1977-78. He spent the next four years playing for Philadelphia before joining Edmonton in 1982.

9.15 C. Montreal's Claude Lemieux

Lemeiux's fame as a playoff standout began long before 1994-95, when he doubled his regular-season goal count of six goals to score 13 playoff markers during New Jersey's Stanley Cup run. His reputation was established in his rookie year, 1985-86, when Lemieux, after just one goal in 10 regular-season games, surprised everyone with 10 goals in 20 postseason games. Montreal won its 23rd Stanley Cup and Lemieux was the playoff sensation. Ciccarelli leads all rookies with 14 goals (1981) and Roenick is second with 11 goals (1991), but neither played as few regular-season games in his rookie year as Lemieux. Roenick had 78 games of experience and Ciccarelli had 32 games against Lemieux's 10-game total.

9.16 C. Eight Cups with three different teams

In 1998, Bowman made history by winning his eighth Stanley Cup, equalling Toe Blake's all-time record. In doing so, the Red Wings head coach also tied Blake and Dick Irvin's record for most games won in the Stanley Cup finals, with 32. Bowman coached Montreal to five Cups in the 1970s, then won another in Pittsburgh in 1992, and added his seventh and eighth on his third championship team, Detroit, in 1997 and 1998.

Scotty Bowman's Playoff Coaching Record*					
Team	Years	Games	Wins	Losses	Cups
St. Louis	4	52	26	26	0
Montreal	8	98	70	28	5
Buffalo	5	36	18	18	0
Pittsburgh	2	33	23	10	1
Detroit	5	86	61	29	2
Total	24	305	198	111	8

*Current to 1998

9.17 A. Two players

Although many players have won Cups with two different teams, only two NHLers since 1943-44 have succeeded in winning a championship on a third team. Larry Hillman won with Detroit (1955), Toronto (1964 and 1967) and Montreal (1969). Claude Lemieux, the only other modern-day three-team Cup champion, captured silver on every team he has played: Montreal (1986), New Jersey (1995) and Colorado (1996).

9.18 D. Eight family members

Amidst the rest of the Red Wings, Ilitch somehow got the names of his entire immediate family engraved on the 1997 Stanley Cup: wife Marian Ilitch; sons Atanas Ilitch, Chris Ilitch, Ron Ilitch and Michael Ilitch Jr.; and daughters Denise Ilitch Lites, Lisa Ilitch Murray and Carole Ilitch Trepeck. Among the nine Ilitches (including owner Mike Sr.) on the Cup, only four (Mike, Marian, Atanas and Chris) are actually managers of the club.

9.19 A. Bobby Orr

The legendary Boston Bruins blueliner won three straight league Hart Trophies as league MVP in the early 1970s. In two of those years (1970 and 1972), Orr also captured the Conn Smythe Trophy as the most valuable playoff performer. No other player has ever managed to win both MVP trophies on more than one occasion.

9.20 C. Detroit's Scotty Bowman
Bowman became the NHL's most successful coach because he knew how to work not only his bench, but the media, too. During the 1998 Conference finals against Dallas, the Red Wings bench boss ranted to the press about the glowing puck used on the FOX telecasts, complaining that the pucks (with the computer chip inside) bounced too much and made for ugly hockey (because they can't be frozen). "I never saw a puck bounce so much. I hope the NHL is researching this puck," fumed Bowman. "If it's only to make a blue streak in the puck, if that's going to make the NHL live for the next 20 years, I've got to be happy. I have a pension coming." NHL senior vice-president Brian Burke shrugged off Bowman's criticism by saying, "If it wasn't that, it would have been something else."

9.21 B. Five captains
When Detroit Red Wings centre Steve Yzerman captured the Conn Smythe Trophy as most valuable player of the 1998 playoffs, he became the fifth captain to receive the coveted award in its 34-year history. The four previous captains to claim the trophy were Joe Sakic of the Colorado Avalanche (1996), Mario Lemieux of the Pittsburgh Penguins (1991 and 1992), Wayne Gretzky of the Edmonton Oilers (1985 and 1988) and Jean Béliveau of the Montreal Canadiens (1965). Somewhat surprisingly, multiple Cup-winning captains such as Denis Potvin and Bobby Clarke never won the Conn Smythe, while Mark Messier and Bob Gainey were voted playoff MVPs, but not when they were captains of their respective teams.

9.22 D. Edmonton's dynasty teams of the 1980s
No playoffs in modern hockey have set or tied as many scoring records as in 1985, when the Oilers won their second straight Stanley Cup. Edmonton players set eight prominent NHL

individual playoff records and the club set four NHL team records, including the mark for most goals by one team in one series (44).

1985's Record-Setting Playoff Records (Individual Records for One Playoff Year)			
Player	**Playoff Record**	**No.**	**Set/Tied**
Wayne Gretzky	Most assists	30	Set record
Wayne Gretzky	Most points	47	Set record
Wayne Gretzky	Most finals goals	7	Tied record
Jari Kurri	Most goals	19	Tied record
Jari Kurri	Most hat tricks	4	Set record
Paul Coffey	Most goals/D-man	12	Set record
Paul Coffey	Most assists/D-man	25	Set record
Paul Coffey	Most points/D-man	37	Set record

SOLUTIONS TO GAMES

Game 1: THE PUCK PUZZLE

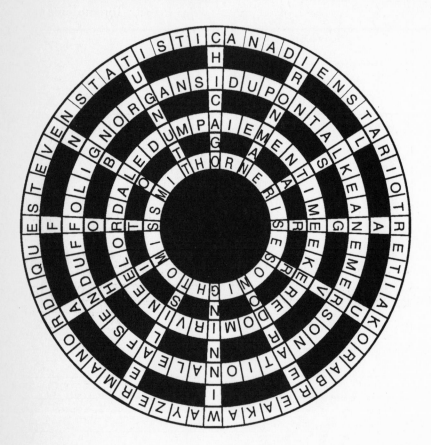

Game 2: SNIPERS OF 1992-93

Among the record 21 players to score 100 or more points in 1992-93, only Mario Lemieux scored his 100th point in 1992. It came in the Penguins' 39th game of the season (a 3-3 tie with Toronto) and the last game of 1992 on New Year's Eve, December 31.

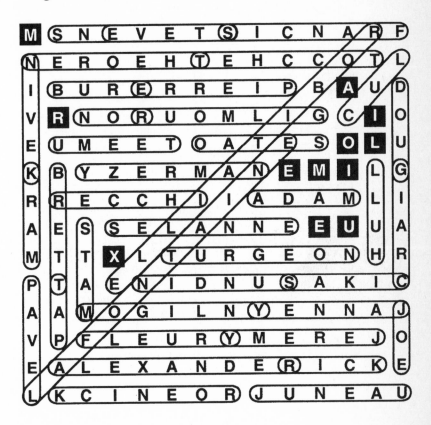

Game 3: TERRIFIC TRIOS

1. Toronto Maple Leafs
2. Boston Bruins
3. Montreal Maroons
4. New York Islanders
5. Detroit Red Wings
6. Los Angeles Kings
7. Buffalo Sabres
8. Vancouver Canucks
9. Philadelphia Flyers
10. New York Rangers
11. Chicago Blackhawks
12. Montreal Canadiens

F. The Kid Line
H. The Nitro Line
J. The S Line
E. The Long Island Lighting Co.
C. The Production Line
B. The Triple Crown Line
G. The French Connection
L. The Life Line
A. The Legion of Doom
I. The GAG Line
D. The Scooter Line
K. The Punch Line

Game 4: NHL DEFECTORS

Part 1
1. Wayne Gretzky
2. Richard Brodeur
3. Anders Hedberg
4. Gordie Roberts
5. Mike Gartner
6. Mark Napier
7. Michel Goulet
8. Dave Langevin
9. Paul Holmgren
10. Mark Howe

H. Indianapolis Racers
G. Quebec Nordiques
E. Winnipeg Jets
D. New England Whalers
F. Cincinnati Stingers
A. Toronto Toros
I. Birmingham Bulls
C. Edmonton Oilers
J. Minnesota Fight Saints
B. Houston Aeros

Part 2

1. Andy Bathgate
2. Norm Ullman
3. Frank Mahovlich
4. Kent Douglas
5. J. C. Tremblay
6. Ted Green
7. Ralph Backstrom
8. Pat Stapleton
9. Reggie Fleming
10. Eric Nesterenko

H. Vancouver Blazers
E. Edmonton Oilers
I. Birmingham Bulls
B. New York Raiders
A. Quebec Nordiques
G. Winnipeg Jets
C. New England Whalers
J. Cincinnati Stingers
F. Chicago Cougars
D. Los Angeles Sharks

Game 5: ART ROSS WINNERS

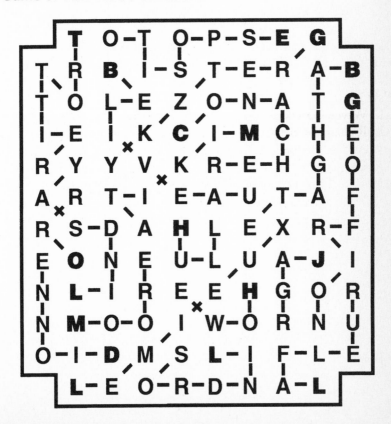

Game 6: TEAM IRONMEN*

1. Anaheim Mighty Ducks	I. Joe Sacco	333 games
2. Boston Bruins	W. Johnny Bucyk	1,436 games
3. Buffalo Sabres	E. Gilbert Perreault	1,191 games
4. Calgary Flames	V. Al MacInnis	803 games
5. Carolina Hurricanes	J. Ron Francis	714 games
6. Chicago Blackhawks	S. Stan Mikita	1,394 games
7. Colorado Avalanche	G. Michel Goulet	813 games
8. Dallas Stars	D. Neal Broten	992 games
9. Detroit Red Wings	M. Gordie Howe	1,687 games
10. Edmonton Oilers	Z. Kevin Lowe	1,037 games
11. Florida Panthers	B. Scott Mellanby	368 games
12. Los Angeles Kings	K. Dave Taylor	1,111 games
13. Montreal Canadiens	F. Henri Richard	1,256 games
14. New Jersey Devils	Y. John MacLean	934 games
15. New York Islanders	L. Bryan Trottier	1,123 games
16. New York Rangers	X. Harry Howell	1,160 games
17. Ottawa Senators	T. Alexandre Daigle	301 games
18. Philadelphia Flyers	A. Bobby Clarke	1,144 games
19. Phoenix Coyotes	P. Thomas Steen	950 games
20. Pittsburgh Penguins	O. Jean Pronovost	753 games
21. St. Louis Blues	N. Bernie Federko	927 games
22. San Jose Sharks	R. Jeff Odgers	334 games
23. Tampa Bay Lightning	Q. Rob Zamuner	417 games
24. Toronto Maple Leafs	H. George Armstrong	1,187 games
25. Vancouver Canucks	C. Stan Smyl	896 games
26. Washington Capitals	U. Kelly Miller	878 games

Games played current to 1997-98

```
B  K-I-M  P  A-S-T-N-Y  T-R-A-G
E  I  R-E  T  R-Q-U  R-E-N  Y  E-L
T  L  R  S  U  L  C-I  E  C  K  R  I-L
A  F  I  E  O  E  I-E  C  Z  A  P-O-R
D-E  A  V  B  M  X-U  T  D-E-R  P  P
R-E  K  U  E  G-R-E  N  H-O-W  S  N
E  K  E  R  L  A  D  A  E-R  K  E  R  O
O  L  N  A  T  R  U  L  I-S-S  U-H  E
Y-K  L  A  L-C  E  A-N  O  E  H  C  I
C-U  E  M-R-E-Z  L  O  M  T  A  R  T
D  B  T  E-U-R  Y  T  C-D  W-E  T
E  A  L  C-H-I-O  M  T  M  S  T-R-O
L  R  C  F  A-M  U  A  I-S  O-P-S  H
V-E  L-A  N  L-L  H-O-V-L-I-C  E
```

Game 8: THE ALL-TIME TOP TWENTY

1. Wayne Gretzky	Q.	1979-80
2. Bobby Orr	M.	1966-67
3. Gordie Howe	D.	1946-47
4. Mario Lemieux	T.	1984-85
5. Maurice Richard	C.	1943-44
6. Doug Harvey	E.	1947-48
7. Jean Béliveau	G.	1953-54
8. Bobby Hull	J.	1957-58
9. Terry Sawchuk	F.	1950-51
10. Eddie Shore	B.	1926-27
11. Guy Lafleur	N.	1971-72
12. Mark Messier	R.	1979-80
13. Jacques Plante	H.	1953-54
14. Ray Bourque	S.	1979-80
15. Howie Morenz	A.	1923-24
16. Glenn Hall	I.	1955-56
17. Stan Mikita	K.	1959-60
18. Phil Esposito	L.	1963-64
19. Denis Potvin	O.	1973-74
20. Mike Bossy	P.	1977-78